BÔ YIN RÂ
(JOSEPH ANTON SCHNEIDERFRANKEN)

THE GATED GARDEN
VOLUME THIRTY-TWO

THE GATED GARDEN

For information
about the books of Bô Yin Râ and
titles available in English translation
visit The Kober Press web site at
http://www.kober.com

THE KOBER PRESS PUBLISHES THE ONLY ENGLISH TRANSLATIONS
OF THE BOOKS OF BÔ YIN RÂ AUTHORIZED BY THE KOBER VERLAG,
SWITZERLAND. THE KOBER VERLAG PUBLISHES THE BOOKS OF
BÔ YIN RÂ IN THE ORIGINAL GERMAN AND HAS PROTECTED
THEIR INTEGRITY SINCE THE AUTHOR'S LIFETIME.

BÔ YIN RÂ
(JOSEPH ANTON
SCHNEIDERFRANKEN)

THE
GATED
GARDEN

TRANSLATED FROM THE GERMAN BY
B.A. REICHENBACH

THE
KOBER
PRESS

BERKELEY, CALIFORNIA

Printed in the United States of America

International Standard Book Number: 978-0-915034-23-9

Typography and composition by Dickie Magidoff

Book cover after a design by Bô Yin Râ

IN MEMORIAM

This translation of the final work of
The Gated Garden
is gratefully dedicated to
Devadatti Schneiderfranken
July 20, 1919-February 20, 2015
daughter of Bô Yin Râ
and life-long, devoted custodian
of his literary and artistic legacy.

CONTENTS

1 Words of Guidance at the Gate. 9

2 On the Simplicity of All that
is Eternal 19

3 On Changing the Point of Perspective,
and on the Concept of "Steps" 27

4 On Levels of Consciousness and
Helping Those Who suffer 35

5 On the Consciousness of
the Departed. 43

6 What a Helper is Risking to Lose 51

7 The Image Mocking the Eternal Self . . 61

8 Once More Concerning Truth
and Reality. 71

9 On Timeless and Temporal Space 77

10 On Insights of Asian Religions. 85

11 On the Mystery of the Orient 93

12 On Religion and Its Forms 101

13 On Giving Consent and the Power
   of Faith 111

14 On Mistaken Images of God 119

15 On the Intent of All Teaching 127

16 Where I Am but the Messenger 135

17 To Whom I Have Nothing to Say 143

18 On the Soul's Eternal Salvation 151

19 How the Urge to Ask Questions
   Delays One's Advance 159

20 On the Timeless and Temporal
   Form of the Soul 165

21 What Survives After Death 173

22 On a Name and a Mere Expedient . . 181

23 Conclusions to be Drawn on
   One's Own 189

24 On Crucial Underestimation 197

25 On the Dilemma of Pastoral Care 205

26 How Everything Eternal is to Itself
   Merely Natural 215

27 Conclusion and Farewell 227

CHAPTER ONE

WORDS OF GUIDANCE AT THE GATE

T O HUMAN BEINGS OF *THIS EARTH*, exclusively depending on the observations transmitted by their brain, and the deductions of their thinking, nearly everything that is *eternal* in their nature, which is to say, can never cease to exist, nor face disintegration however imagined, in truth remains a *hortus conclusus**, a Gated Garden. That such a realm exists, inaccessible alike to physical senses, as well as to efforts of thought, may well be at times suspected, at times also felt, and among large groups of people *believed*; but those who in this way suspect, or feel, or believe, remain outside the wall that separates the garden of

---

*Hortus Conclusus is the title of the German original of this book, and the collective, symbolic title of the author's thirty-two volume cycle of Spiritual Guidance. The term "hortus conclusus" is from the Vulgate text of The Song of Songs.

their own eternal nature's consciousness—the paradise lost—which is closed to them, and thus beyond the domains of knowledge made possible by physical senses. Some, who still are not satisfied with all they suspect, feel, and believe, now tirelessly walk around that wall they cannot scale, constantly probing for a hidden crack they still might possibly find, which could be enlarged, allowing them to squeeze through. The most fortunate among such seekers, to their great surprise, actually come to the only true portal, which is difficult to find, but could become the entry to the gated garden, if only they knew how to open it. But instead of patiently waiting, and trusting that one day perhaps it might be unlocked from inside, nearly all fortunate enough to have discovered the portal seek to get hold of the most curious counterfeit keys from sly locksmiths; and so they waste their life on earth with ever new, but constantly fruitless efforts to force from without the lock of the gated garden, which cannot be opened, except from within. In vain is their labor, and ill-fated self-deception.

Only one who himself is conscious of eternal life, and, by virtue of his spiritual nature, has his home in the gated garden, which is inexorably barred to all earthly intrusiveness, is able to open the mysterious portal *from within*; yet even having thus been opened, that portal admits no one but those who cast from them all burdening weights of mental speculation, and every external disguise they had used, in order to enter naked and free, as their mothers had brought them to life.

The work of my entire life is a constantly renewed opening of that portal, brought about from within; and from here I then guide all who want to take no more with them than what belongs to life eternal in their nature, and lead them by manifold paths to the temples I built for the teachings they hold, and to the pillars I raised, inscribed with words teaching truths that are valid forever.

Every teaching conveyed to my fellow human beings through me is surrounded by the wall of this *gated garden*, so that I may rightly and fittingly leave my entire work of spiritual guidance to posterity under this name, which also includes myself. For good reasons I judge it appropriate symbolically to name likewise the present final volume of my writings. Also this book makes available to many readers specific answers that in the course of past decades I had privately given to individuals; and like the volume *Letters to One and Many*, it is meant to open the eyes of those who were led to my books and trust them, to make them see that the books and writings in which can be found what I have to convey from realms of the Eternal, must be regarded as a unified whole that is rooted in the Eternal, and can become accessible only if the conditions are met which the Eternal imposes. I have often enough spoken of those conditions, and once again characterized them in the foregoing remarks.

The locations toward which in this present book I now still intend to guide those who are called, into the inner parts of this garden, which is forever barred to all idle curiosity are sites that offer manifold views of orientation from its sacred groves, which display, in clearest perspective, the architectural structure of the temples I erected to shelter their teachings. Also some steles and inscribed pillars will no longer escape the attentive eye in their unintentional concealment.

I truly know how alien the teachings offered in my writings must appear to nearly all of my fellow human beings; and I understand only too well that people today, devoid of experience in eternal dimensions, initially remain incapable correctly to absorb into their conceptualizing faculties, instilled by education, what I regrettably am forced to tell them also about myself, if I am not to leave them standing before blank spaces which they are unable to fill in through their own knowledge. No less am I acquainted with the various kinds of psychologically masked suspicions, which irresponsible hastiness keeps in readiness for everything it finds inexplicable, as the most convenient way to hide its own ignorance. In view of the innumerable mental speculations dealing with eternal things, I surely understand that one remains unwilling to accept that any of one's fellow mortals might possibly be able, protected from all self-deception, lucidly to experience his own being within the realm that is beyond all doubt eternal.

All real understanding is additionally obstructed by many primitive religious concepts, adopted not only by highly developed religions, but, proceeding from theological areas of thinking, surprisingly are able to cling with weed-like tenacity also in brains whose owners deem themselves far removed from dogmas of all kinds. No less obstructive are the intellectual impediments that, like gigantic creeping vines thriving on putrid soil in tropical jungles, prevent all perception of the authentic Eternal in the domain of philosophical systems.

Under such conditions, here touched upon only briefly, it becomes a quite painful task as a human among humans to state that, excluding very few others, but of non-European cultural background, who remain in strictest seclusion, one personally is an exponent of eternal Reality in the domain of humans on earth. And in addition, to have been inescapably called upon, from the eternal dimension, to convey, as the only translator into human language on earth, what can become known exclusively by means of wordless experience. Truly, one must have learned simply to laugh within oneself at any kind of need, whether hidden or obvious, to feel important, if in one's earthly, time-restricted existence one is not to despair of being able to fulfill such a task. Solely unlimited love for all that is eternally worthy of love, which one sees given in each of one's fellow human beings, even though in most of them it barely is conscious, is able to create the energy to open oneself again and again from within the Eternal, despite being aware that even so, for most of one's fellow mortals, one is bound to remain a closed "gated garden."

❧

CHAPTER TWO

ON THE SIMPLICITY OF ALL THAT IS ETERNAL

THE MELLOWNESS OF ETERNAL SPIRITUAL LIGHT is not perceived by over-stimulated nerves. Only in the previously gained quiet serenity of the soul, which remains undisturbed, can the golden-white radiance of the Godhead reveal itself to human experience on earth.

I truly may speak with innermost spiritual authority about the way that life is lived and experienced in the eternal Spirit, such as is possible only for those who know that experience themselves. But for that very reason I must affirm that even in the highest sphere of spiritual life, which is part, however, of my consciousness as tangible experience, there reigns the identical sober, lucid simplicity, and inherent necessity, familiar to everyone who even once in this earthly life had consciously known eternal Reality, at any level whatever.

The images most people have of life in the eternal Spirit, and how the human being experiences this spiritual existence, are so profoundly colored by earthly impressions, and so complicated in conception, that this effectively *prevents* any genuine experience in the realm of the Spirit. But all who once had faced the inexpressible inherent necessity, and the sober, lucid simplicity of spiritual Life, and how it is experienced, having thus been moved to the depth of their being, will doubtless understand why I warn against forming any fantastical notions that would decide in advance how spiritual Life *ought* to present itself to humans on earth.

I truly have created, for every form within the timeless substance of the Spirit that lends itself to verbal presentation, a faithful reflection through words, shielding with silence only such domains of the structure of spiritual Life that transcend all comparison, and thus every rendition in physical language. But the most exalted mystery of even those domains is protected by their indescribable simplicity, unimaginable in physical terms; the inherent necessity, beyond every question, of the events one may behold in these spheres. Experienced here is nothing unsettling, agitating, bewildering, frightening, let alone "spooky," but worlds of absolute spiritual clarity that exclude anything nebulous, questionable, and uncertain. Such is the state in all dimensions of fully conscious, inner, eternal Life in the Spirit's radiant substance and, consequently, also in the timeless soul of a mortal, wherein a Luminary of primordial Light imparts his life, within the span of time allotted him on earth.

The Luminary of primordial Light, however, is united with the eternal soul of one who is offered him in life on earth, for the sole reason that only by virtue of such union can also other eternal souls that experience and structure themselves, in human beings on earth, in physical time, be granted the "gift from on high"—the timeless energy of Light, born of the Spirit—which they need in order to attain their awakening in consciousness everlasting. The teachings I convey in words, as a Luminary of primordial Light, may thus become the initial motivation for many, by their own partaking of feelings and impressions, gradually to prepare themselves for the awakening of their eternal soul; seen from the Spirit's realm of radiant substance, however, my simply being *spiritually present* in the midst of earthly life, is far more consequential than all my conscious activity. And in respect to the latter it must be noted that the teachings, embodied in words, and thus made visually discernible, constitute in truth only the smallest part of what I am bound to effect from the Spirit's dimension.

By far the greatest difficulty in my intentional work, however—both in the realm of the soul, and when conveying spiritual teachings in words—is the discrepancy between the increasingly more self-complicating complexity of the mentally conditioned shaping of concepts, and the physically incomprehensible simplicity of Life in the eternal Spirit's radiant substance. Above all in the realm of language a chasm must here be crossed that can be bridged only by using the materials of the mental world of earthly concepts and thinking, ruled by the most complex distinctions. Given that all words of any human language —without exception—are unsuited to serve as tools to express or convey the primordial quintessence of simplicity, one must resort to the most complicated mental images and concepts if, via the byway of language, one intends to bring feelings close to physical sensibility, which it would be unable to experience if it had no means to awaken them in its own complicated intellectual way. If the bridge thus created, however, is truly to connect what seems eternally separated, one must not foolishly attempt to dissolve, by philosophical acids, the material drawn from the store of mentally fashioned complexity, which is solely to make crossing the chasm possible, as it only holds up as long as corrosive thought will not dismantle it. A bridge is built to let one cross it, not to be taken apart under one's feet.

I truly know only too well what the soul of someone must bear, who is at home in the free, primordial simplicity of the Eternal, and whose psycho-physical organism, which perceives sensations, is liberated from the bondage that normally would be its state on earth, when being forced to endure all the multitudes of literally diabolical vibrations reverberating through the living space of present-day Western civilization, which is close to suffocating in its progressively more complicated ways. However, the impossibility of letting eternal spiritual Life in its radiant substance effectively manifest itself in its unparalleled simplicity within that civilization's dimension of life, except by sharing this physical life on the part of a Luminary of primordial Light, shoulders me—as the one born to this end at this time—with the categorical obligation of taking part in this life; a duty I never could truly fulfill if—united only with those who, eternally born like myself in the Spirit, I now call my spiritual Brothers—I sought to distance, or permanently to sever myself from the domains of external life, in which my European fellow mortals, and those who live according to Western customs in the rest of the world, are enmeshed.

Even so, however, I need to reserve for myself a degree of relative isolation within the domains of this complex Western civilization, which, to be sure, is not by any means to be renounced root and branch, if I am to be able spiritually to fulfill everything that duty compels me to do, by sharing the lives of those who live at this time; since day by day these obligations call for ample hours of unconditionally offered solitude.

❧

CHAPTER THREE

ON CHANGING THE POINT OF PERSPECTIVE, AND ON THE CONCEPT OF "STEPS"

THERE IS NO LEVEL IN SPIRITUAL LIFE AT which one might have to forgo once more to assume the same state of mind in which one had been when first attempting to set foot on the lowest of steps. One may approach everything one encounters, and which moves our soul, freely, without hesitation, again and again, as if one had not received any teachings, nor experienced the least in the timeless realm of the Spirit.

Indeed, it may be quite beneficial from time to time to practice this change of position, even without special reason. Much as artists, after each further perfection of a painting, are used to stepping back from the canvas on which they are working, so as to judge, by viewing all parts of the work as a whole, what still remains to be done, even so should those preparing themselves to receive eternal spiritual Light, from time to time gain distance from themselves, in order to grow aware of what they still lack for gaining the sought ability to receive spiritual Light. Besides, stepping back from oneself, and from insights already attained, will unexpectedly strengthen what has been achieved at this point.

One would be greatly mistaken, however, assuming that here I offer advice whose practice one easily may recommend to another, after being oneself removed from the like. On the contrary, I can hardly imagine a day on which my consciousness, descending from my highest, innermost eternal point of perspective, would not explore all intermediate levels anew, down to the lowest creature-consciousness of the impermanent physical body, which I "consume" in life on this earth.

Having returned again from such depth into my eternal Being, I am able to feel, and thus to gauge, what in each case needs to be done from the Spirit's dimension. If I were never to leave the highest state of my Being, I would not be who I am, from Eternity, in the *eternally present moment*, from which I was able to enter earthly time only by having dared the risk of seeking out what solely he can "know" who consciously within himself experiences also the profoundest depth. And thus *I am*: the Luminary in primordial Light, even as *I am* a self who once more gained his consciousness within the timeless Spirit, as one of those who fell, through their own fault, into the realm of earthly time; and lastly, in physically effected appearance, *I am* also the mortal earthly human in a creature body. The number of steps descending from my own highest state to my lowest is far greater, however, than this summary sketch might lead one to think. But here one cannot offer details because it could not create understanding. Only those who, as Luminaries of primordial Light, are enabled on their own to descend from, and then once more to ascend that ladder of steps, a capacity denied the human self as such, know of their differentiated nature. Nor would such knowledge be of use to any other consciousness.

I speak of all these things in order to root out, at the very outset, the foolish notion that it might be "unbecoming" to admit to still being conscious of feelings that recall the concerns of one's beginnings, so that this idea may never sprout again. If necessity demands that each and every day I leave the highest state of my eternal spiritual consciousness, so that by sharing I am able to experience the fate of souls who live within the lowest hellish depths on earth, then truly no one seeking Light need be concerned if occasionally feeling as if still at the first of steps.

The blessing from eternal Light would lead them back again to the highest level of their present consciousness—and greatly enriched by inner perceptiveness—even if at times they had to behold themselves abysmally beneath the insights already fathomed on the very first step of their path. For the steps of this path are not levels of "rank" from which one might be hurled, but exclusively degrees of insight and enlightenment; and it is left entirely up to seekers themselves whether and when they decide on occasion to return to an earlier level of insight, in order to relive it in memory, and then, when ascending once more, to experience anew what had already been granted them in its entirety. The entire path of these steps is one of constantly growing inner awareness. For that reason, every step that has been ascended becomes a permanent possession, not merely for all time, but for Eternity. And this possession would remain in existence even if, through guilt caused on earth, it would have to become in-accessible to the individual's consciousness for aeons. But fortunately, only very few tend to confront a fate so unspeakably sad.

⁓

CHAPTER FOUR

ON LEVELS OF CONSCIOUSNESS AND HELPING THOSE WHO SUFFER

I T SURELY IS NEVER AN EASY DECISION voluntarily to relinquish the contents of a consciousness that earthly means cannot hope to describe—given that all the clichés like "absolute harmony," "purest clarity," "ultimate bliss," do not even remotely approach its wealth—and step by step to descend, through ever less enlightened regions, until at last one is able to perceive once again the dull inertia of the human being's purely animal existence; and yet in all of that is also found so great a wealth of experience for someone who is still connected with the earth, and consequently able to measure yet by earthly scales, that I regard it as a "grace" to be obligated to explore this path each day anew.

On this daily descent into darkness, and returning again into Light, one's soul must of necessity also share all the suffering endured in these regions of varying levels of darkness. Such would be unbearable, had not my soul been taught and developed to that end; if thus I did not at the same time also see, in every form of suffering, the hidden *lie* at work, and did not know of the quite certain future *reevaluation* of all suffering. I must admit, however, that I am able consciously to share all the horrors of such suffering, which at times by far surpasses the personal physical suffering I know only too well, solely by gathering every last energy of my soul; and the vibrations caused by such sharing often still echo painfully for days in my physical consciousness, despite their having been instantly dissolved in the realm of the Spirit. Yet what does all my voluntary sharing—as suffering felt in the soul as my own—amount to, compared to the measureless floods of suffering involuntarily endured as such in all dimensions of consciousness, without ceasing! It would truly be diabolical indifference in the face of what other individual souls are compelled to endure, if one of those who have knowledge that suffering here must be shared, if relief shall be offered, were to refrain from

thus taking part in what is endured; and, truly,
there is no "merit" in here not sparing one

 that opens itself from without. One must be
willing to be conscious in it, for a time, according to its own inherent ways, if one is to
be able to bring help within the bounds of its
dominion.

In view of everything I have already stated
elsewhere to clarify these matters, I hardly
need to add here that this voluntary sharing
every day of the most differing domains of
consciousness, which are not part of my own
normal state of being conscious, does not in
any way involve a change of actual location;
and that all such sharing of life that is suffered in each of these different realms of consciousness implies a *general* acceptance of
the particular "vibrations" of suffering that
are actually effective in the particular realm.
Shared in this way is the suffering primarily
felt by all those tormented in a particular
sphere, without any unfolding, however, of
the individual fates within which such suffering is endured. The help provided consists in
the release of the spiritual energies requested
in each case, which then become effective,

without any further direction within the respective dimensions of consciousness, wherever they are most needed. Accordingly, each case will thus be granted energy enabling further endurance of suffering, or to provide relief, liberation, or in some other form as required.

Such sharing of others' lives and lending them effective help, is possible, however, only at the price of an extraordinary depletion of physical energies. Often it is necessary to consume more vital energies in a few hours than people engaged in the most intensive form of external physical, or intellectually demanding life are able to use up in many months. What has been given away when performing work in the spiritual realm is of necessity irretrievably lost to the helper's physical energy. Compared to performing work in the domain of spiritual substance, the most strenuous labor in temporal life is bound to feel like recreation, but one cannot do one as well as the other; and what is consumed in purely spiritual work is irreplaceably missing in physical life. By contrast, any energies that stream from the domain of the Eternal, but which may be transformed into the earthly realm, will here not lead by any means to an increase of physical energy, but solely create the possibility of an otherwise impossible level of heightened consumption of physically given energies in the eternal dimension. It is most definitely not the case that spiritual Reality has no need of a temporal agent. That alone which the Luminary of primordial Light is able, during his life on earth, to keep free for performing his work in eternal dimensions, can he direct to where he would offer spiritual help, or prevent avoidable suffering; no matter what burdens his own earthly life may force him to bear, which, owing to its very nature, is in effect a life lived only for others, without question, or choice.

CHAPTER FIVE

ON THE
CONSCIOUSNESS
OF THE DEPARTED

THE CONSTANTLY REPEATED EXPLORING OF A substantial series of the most diverse levels of consciousness, which is part of my voluntarily accepted, daily spiritual obligations, naturally also includes the spheres of consciousness of those who have departed from the earth. Yet here, too, there is no possible exception that might allow one to identify the fate of a particular individual.

Not so long ago, however, there was a time when I found myself able—intermittently, and in ways very difficult to endure, under certain rare conditions, which by no means depended on me alone—briefly to come into contact also with individually defined souls who had departed from the earth, within their respective regions of consciousness. This resulted from the psycho-physical after-effect,

by no means desired, and certainly not intended by either side, of particular necessi-
ties, connected with my earlier spiritual-bodily
schooling of many years. That sensibility
caused me intense suffering, also bodily, as
the entire situation demanded an enormous
commitment of energies to remain equal to it.
I thus was indeed able, in some individual
cases, to bring authentic comfort to people
who had lost souls very dear to them, but the
mediation between those visibly living on
earth, and such as have left the visible realm,
is not something intended for either the physical cosmos, nor in the spiritual universe, and
least of all could I be the one to perform such
a task. Thus, I was very glad when I one day
no longer needed any defensive resistance,
and then more and more clearly noticed how
this unwanted state of an unintentional sensi-
tivity began to subside. But even more was
I pleased when at last I was able to terminate
it altogether. And I certainly do not deplore
having lost it.

Concerning the ways a Luminary of primordial Light may have contact with human souls
removed from the earth there regrettably pre-
vail fantastic notions even in the heads of

otherwise quite sensible and open-minded people. The only correct assumption made in this context is that we are able to share feelings in the domains where those are conscious who have physically "died." What this actually means, however, one fails completely to grasp; for it implies nothing less than being able, within the domains where the dead are conscious, to perceive oneself as having *in fact* physically "died."

Instead, even people who elsewhere display quite rational judgment assume without thinking, that it must be an easy matter, among numberless millions of souls, who in innermost beatific concentration are absorbed in their spiritually given Light, and would resent being "called" as a painful intrusion, literally to "summon," as it were, a particular, identifiable soul, in order to conduct the equivalent of an otherworldly "interview."

That people having suffered loss hard to endure, through the parting from the world of physical senses of loved ones closely bound to their hearts, may become absurdly naïve, is shown in ways both shocking and pathetic by the startling numbers of believers in "mediumism," whether they still call themselves "spiritualists," or, since the term has become somewhat disreputable, have adopted a different, but equally misleading description. Among readers of my books offering guidance, who regard themselves as my pupils, one truly should not have to be confronted with that degree of cluelessness concerning spiritual matters; but even in these no doubt sufficiently instructed circles one still comes across occasional readers for whom *The Book on Life Beyond* seems not to exist; nor anything else I communicated in so many other passages that deal with that topic.

The only class of departed one might encounter in the way imagined by the naïve credulity described above would be the truly pitiable souls who still spook about in the various *border realms* they have themselves created. But these are so deeply under the spell of their own creation that they do not want to, and therefore cannot experience anything other than what they have formed, through their own faith, as the sole reality they seek to experience, and which they project into their "outer" surroundings. We are unable to make them aware of us before they have exhausted the energies of faith they brought with them from earthly life; and that may take a very long time. Human souls who, millennia before our era, had lived in a body on earth remain confined within their self-formed *border realms* to this day. Nor will there take place any "mass-awakening," given the dissolution of these collective domains, generated by misdirected energies of faith, occurs, even under best conditions, only intermittently, as a result of the awakening of individuals, one after another, repeated again and again. But having already published enough on the subject, I hardly can add any more explanations.

How one actually remains in contact with those who in earthly life have been taken from us, for our material perception, I likewise have taught very clearly, so that I need merely refer to what has already been given. We Luminaries of primordial Light, however, are able to help the departed who can in fact be reached, solely through offering guidance and Light in other than personal ways.

❧

CHAPTER SIX

ON WHAT
A HELPER IS
RISKING TO LOSE

WHEN DESCENDING TO LOWER DOMAINS OF consciousness, it is not the "dangers" objectively existing in the structure of these realms, which may cause the Luminary of primordial Light any concerns. Against threats of that nature, one who is conscious in the Spirit's world knows how to protect himself, wherever he might encounter them. What despite that, however, is seeking, again and again, to fill him with horror, as soon as he descends to levels of consciousness, which require a temporary forfeiture of the state of consciousness intrinsic to his Being, is the inexorable knowledge that he thereby divests himself for a certain time of his own spiritual power, and thus remains for that time without defense against a possible "ambush" by destructive forces of the unseen dimensions of the physical world. And such knowledge also includes awareness that subjective impulses of ruination constantly lie in wait for the opportune moment to unleash such attacks against every Luminary of primordial Light whom they can reach in the physically accessible dimension. By contrast, human beings on the lowest level of consciousness, but which at the time is their given condition, remain protected against any attack by destructive tendencies from the physical world, as long as they are able to keep their own will and feelings free of similar drives of destruction. The Luminary of primordial Light, on the other hand, who, by an act of fully conscious will, resolves to enter a sphere of consciousness to which by nature he does not belong, is able to do this only if, for a certain time he detaches himself from his intrinsic spiritual consciousness, and thus will forgo, during that time, the spiritual form that is truly his, in order to experience a lower form as his own. In doing this he necessarily must keep himself "disarmed," a fact of which those invisible destroyers and their visible thralls are fully aware, since the physical activity of every Luminary of primordial Light results in a severe restriction of their own time-determined existence.

Thus, every descent of this kind *apparently* becomes a brazenly daring folly. And even though, when viewed from life on earth, one compares one's descent with all the dangers of everyday life, encountered a thousand times—dangers that numberless human beings throughout the world are forced to risk day after day, already on their way to work; not counting all those whose very profession is full of dangers, demanding fearless calm at all times—the decisive difference remains the measureless worth of the loss that is risked; for the dangers of everyday life in a large city, or in a profession exposed to perils, may certainly threaten the life of the physical body, but could never affect the *spiritual consciousness* of one's own eternal existence, attained during life here on earth. By contrast, the Luminary of primordial Light here needs to fear nothing less than the loss of his spiritually conscious *physical Being*. And none of them knows with certainty in advance whether he will be able, until the end of his temporal life, to regain, again and again, the consciousness of himself as a human being on earth, or whether his earthly self will not in the end be lost to his spiritual Being, so that on earth nothing is left of him but a demented shell, or an imbecile caricature of his true Being. This is the *real* danger that, until the end of his earthly existence, threatened each one who brought Light into life on this earth. Weighed against that, what could any conceivable danger of body and soul ever mean? It is a mere *nothing* compared to the loss that here is at stake, day after day until the last breath of life. Neither from the perspective of eternal spiritual life, nor from that of earthly human existence, seeking contentment in the limited span of physical time, is there indeed any justification to enter that state of danger, where it is not demanded unconditionally, so that absolutely needed spiritual help may be offered, through which alone eternal Love is able once more to communicate with consciousness that would be otherwise beyond its reach.

I hardly still need to say that such danger can never, of course, come near other human beings on earth, no matter what heights of insight they might already be able to reach; for even if they wanted to, they could not withdraw themselves from the domain of consciousness they had already attained, in order to experience themselves, fully awake, in spheres of consciousness far removed from the Spirit.

Dreams may no doubt enmesh in the nets of one of the countless *border realms*, which constantly influence also fully awake human life in its drives and emotions, unless human beings protect themselves with categorically clear directives deciding what they are willing to accept of influences from the unseen dimension, and what should be firmly repelled. But even if whatever was dreamed may have been as vivid as the most impressive experience while being awake, it nonetheless was never anything more than a *dream*, because—fortunately—only the Luminaries of primordial Light are able fully awake to perceive the various kinds of accumulated consciousness, which I have described as *border realms* of the world of life beyond. This exclusion alone sheds light on what one should make of all the real or imagined "clairvoyants," and similar types, who readily furnish "experiences on spiritual planes," without so much as suspecting that not even the said *border realms* are open to them as a fully awake experience, although states of trance and dreaming may on occasion allow them to gain semi-conscious awareness.

In this context I also would like to correct still another error that appears to be something like property commonly shared, so that I am not surprised to find it among the luggage of all human opinions. The erroneous notion in this case expects that in all conditions of life beyond, everything felt, discerned, and experienced must be commonly shared by all who are conscious on the same level of consciousness, so that every individual differentiation is eliminated. Yet that idea is simply one of the numerous mentally fashioned insights that humans on earth construed to make life beyond comprehensible to their understanding. In Reality, however, things are very different; for here each state of conscious life beyond embraces infinite distinctions in individual possessions. What does not exist in the experience of life beyond, however, is any chance of disguising oneself before others, made possible on earth by the human's animal nature; nor can anyone here assume importance not in accord with genuine merit.

I must warn, however, against letting one's thoughts dwell too much on the nature of life beyond. What one already knows about it through me is more than sufficient so to determine this impermanent earthly existence that it must yield its truly not insignificant energies of resonance, in order to make it possible that those who seek may reliably come to know the characteristics of life beyond, even here and now.

❧

CHAPTER SEVEN

THE IMAGE
MOCKING THE
ETERNAL SELF

IF BOTH IN MEDIAEVAL, AND IN THE SO MUCH older Oriental mysticism, the turning away from, indeed, the inner extinction of the Self, is made a demand, I may surely say of myself that there has scarcely been any "mystic" on earth who could know of himself with such certainty that this impermanent Self had been burned out in him to the very last spark, as —from the perspective of my conscious eternal spiritual Being—I know this about myself with absolute clarity. If I nonetheless say in the texts of my Guidance that the sage is Self from his depth, and that everything within him is ruled by his Self, it should be obvious that by the same word I mean something other than what the respective mystics had in mind. Indeed, I speak of something completely *opposite*; namely, the eternal *primordial form*, originating in the eternal Spirit, whose distorted pretense in animal-fettered life the masters of mysticism exclusively meant in their writings. I truly do not warn against treating this mask with contempt, which uses the name of "self." Unfortunately, it enjoys such high repute throughout the world and among all peoples that hardly any who identify themselves with it are even aware of how in this way they merely ape their genuine self. No wonder that only so very few people are willing to abandon the deceptive image, which is the inexorable condition for attaining consciousness in the primordial form of the *spiritual self*. Far too enamored of the self-created pseudo-image of their genuine self, people are so profoundly convinced of its actual earthly importance, of the significance, real or assumed, accorded this pseudo-image, and thus are not inclined to persuade themselves to give up what they know, and is seemingly so secure, for the sake of something presumably so uncertain as the eternal form of their own *primordial self*.

Human beings no longer know that what they bundle together by means of the concept and word "I" is nothing more than something physically *taken on*; features, however, they were able to *take on* solely because the primordial spiritual scintilla "I"—which imbues them with life—offers them the unconscious model that allows them to mold the representation of themselves that most closely reflects their physical inclinations; and thus they themselves impose on their mind the deceptive concept they have formed of their genuine *self*.

An infant on the threshold of exploring its environment in the earliest stages does not yet know what it means when a voice in its surroundings says "I." To itself, the child is still *environment*, in which, as its little everyday experience demonstrates, all things apparently are connected with a particular combination of sounds. Thus it also hears a specific combination of sounds always brought in connection with its own self-expressions, and thus learns to identify its "name" with itself in its environment, in exactly the same way as a young animal may, when it lives close to humans. But when the child, alone among all animals having the gift of a differentiated language, wants to refer to itself, it will call that part of its environment, which it knows as itself, by saying the "name" it has heard again and again to describe it. Only much later does it mechanically learn, by imitation, to say "I," and thus gradually comes to understand that this seems to be the "name" all have in common when they speak of themselves. But even though the child will henceforth also say "I" to itself, the horizon and the depth its consciousness embraces is thereby not affected in the least, despite the fact the adults consider the usage of the personal pronoun they themselves hold in such high regard on the part of the little being as a tremendous step forward.

For the adolescent, and later the grown-up human being, all experience of life resembles a mosaic-like configuration of countless separate things, which once had been part of the surrounding world, until they could be incorporated in the concept of self, now called "I," developed already in childhood. And if among the many separate things the mosaic "I" also includes the belief in a continuation of consciousness beyond death, then nothing seems more obvious to the self-consciousness in that "I" than the fact that all the contents mingled together in the course of its life must be entitled to claim "eternal" duration.

But when at last the abysmal naiveté of this notion is consciously recognized, the shock proves so unbearable that all the other content of self-consciousness detaches itself, in forms either brusque or lamenting, not only from the formerly held belief, but also from any possibility of lending that content a foundation less easily threatened. A critical examination of the individual stones of the mosaic in view of their potentially eternal validity, and a radical elimination of everything doubtless impermanent from the content of the self-asserting consciousness, appears not merely as an imposition impossible to meet, but also entirely hopeless. After all, one also has lost every touchstone fit to determine what is begotten of eternity, and what is merely temporal and impermanent; as a result, one now feels sure to be on solid ground only by summarily ascribing *everything* to the impermanence of earthly existence.

Thus do "believers," no less than those having lost their "belief," make a mockery of the *eternal self*, to which alone they owe not being mere animals, but also *human individuations*; because the *human being* does not have its roots on earth, but in the heart of Eternity—in the innermost of Godhead, whose highest image of Itself is *human* in its Being. In order that the human being's flesh and blood be penetrated by the timeless *self* in its reality, instead of by its mocking imitation, there truly is no need, however, from the perspective of eternal life, that consciousness be purified of everything not *timeless* in its origin. The requirement, instead, is that one will inexorably differentiate between timeless and temporal content. For a long time there is need of constant vigilance, lest inadvertently, perhaps tomorrow, there once more may take root within the innermost of consciousness— within the *timeless self*—what had been barred from it, and only yesterday appeared eradicated. It is like seeking to transform a pasture overgrown with weeds into an orderly garden of precious plants. First the soil needs to be ploughed again and again, and ruthlessly cleared by the rake until it is thoroughly free of everything that earlier had drained its strength. But after the new plants have been sown it still will require watchfulness for some time, lest that grow back again what had been rooted out, but which birds and the wind never fail sowing anew.

All this is not performed by the mind, but labor accomplished in ways that are *felt*, by means of the sharp-edged ploughshare and the sturdy spade of mysterious steel, no usage can blunt, being tempered exclusively in the flame of the soul's innermost *feeling*. Regrettably, however, one still allows at first the mental pseudo-insights, familiar from early days, to grow unchecked within. And that is the reason why many from time to time feel the need to construe for themselves—in place of the Reality, which is solely attained through *experience*—a preliminary, mentally assembled surrogate, which later proves an obstacle in the objective perception of Reality, toward which they once had meant to clear their path.

❧

CHAPTER EIGHT

ONCE MORE CONCERNING TRUTH AND REALITY

(Refers to Chapter Four in *The Path to God*)

*T*RUTH IS NOT THE SAME AS REALITY OF *spiritual substance*, although every *Truth* is rooted in *Reality*. Truth is always an "image" of Reality, even though, as claimed by the word, under all circumstances a precisely graven likeness, in which only such retouching with burin and scraping iron can be condoned that further serves more clearly to show and to heighten that likeness. But while this image will always remain but an "image," and is never *Reality of spiritual substance itself*, the latter remains the eternal cause of knowing Truth, in every form. Saying this, I am by no means playing a game with words. The two concepts signify concrete differences that need to be very clearly distinguished. Much that is related to this subject has already been said in the book *The Path to God*.

When I speak of eternal *Reality*, whose essence is spiritual substance, I want this understood as being the realm that physical senses on earth do not apprehend; that which is Life in itself, at all times *eternal*; the realm Jesus called "the kingdom of heaven"; the domain of the Spirit's radiant substance, which alone in itself encompasses all permanence, as the sole, inexhaustible sum of all energies—which has nothing to do with "thinking," is not a construct of "thought," but: *Eternity-begotten space.* Few things obstruct the way toward finding this eternal Reality within oneself with more tenacious virulence than the fateful, paralyzing habit of using the word "spirit" when speaking of activities within the mortal brain: of thoughts and their interconnections; of mental work, and intellectual life.* Accustomed to using the word "spirit" as a term for such cerebral vapor, whirled up by means of the physical brain, it truly becomes difficult to make one's consciousness capable of receiving the *Creator Spiritus*, which of its own Self *is* sovereign Life everlasting, embracing everything within

---

*This passage refers specifically to speakers of German, who commonly equate the word "Geist" with intellect.

the substance of its Being that is begotten of its realm, but will not receive within itself whatever had not from Eternity proceeded from its substance. Only because, in their *physically inapprehensible core*, human beings are, from all Eternity, the Spirit's timeless progeny—having let themselves fall, from the state of *permanent presence* into the deceptive pseudo-duration of cosmic "time," —are they able one day to enter again the realm of the Spirit; taking with them from their temporal consciousness what they want to retain, to the extent it does not conflict with the laws that govern that realm.

Compared to this Reality, the image lending it form—the Truth—is a likeness minted on earth: Eternity's seal imprinted on temporal wax. The human being, however, that does not bear the eternal seal of the Spirit within itself cannot convey the Truth from the realm of eternal Reality, even if it wanted to with all its physical energies, and all the might of its soul. At issue here is not the well-intentioned human urge "to speak the truth," but bearing witness of being oneself imprinted by timeless Reality. And only one who in this way bears Truth from eternal Reality within him is able to bear witness of the Truth; because his own consciousness became radiant, and is alive, in the Truth imprinted upon him.

❧

CHAPTER NINE

ON TIMELESS AND TEMPORAL SPACE

THAT MATHEMATICIANS IN THE FIELD OF scientifically pursued geometry quite seriously, and not by any means entangled in occultist creeds, accept the possibility of four-dimensional space relationships, indeed, do not consider multi-dimensional spaces as something impossible, is common knowledge among the informed. No one will need to feel guilty of fostering inexcusable fantasies when regarding it as certain that these calculations find their corresponding, equally valid factual proofs in cosmic space as a whole, as do the astronomical calculations of stellar bodies, which remain invisible to the mightiest of telescopes, although their existence and locations are conclusively demonstrated by observing their respective environment.

But all the spaces that may be geometrically deduced remain concealed, as it were, within the three-dimensional space we are able to experience, even though, as three-dimensional beings, we are not able to perceive the four-up to "n"-dimensional spatial configurations and entities. This impossibility of physically perceiving the more than three-dimensional kinds of space, introduced as concepts by geometrical reasoning, must not by any means mislead us to assume that these spaces are anything other than part of the unseen physical world. With that which I speak of as the "space" eternally begotten of the timeless Spirit, all these geometrically conceivable spaces have nothing whatever in common. The Eternal lies beyond the reach of everything that can be calculated, or may be found by methods of thinking; and while it occupies the same place as the physical world, it is completely unimaginable in terms of spatial concepts that may be physically measured.

Nonetheless, geometry, with its intellectual unlocking of multi-dimensional space is very close to shedding light on certain critically observed "meta-psychic" phenomena, which nowadays can be denied by only the most stubborn ignoramus. If this could be done, it also would explain the notoriously mindless nature of so many "spiritualist" manifestations by the lemurian entities in the realm of the physical world that three-dimensional eyes cannot see; events that would be shown as resulting of necessity, because the lemurian phantoms found in action in three-dimensional space are strangers in that dimension.

The entire universe is permeated with spatial dimensions, which normally do not perceive each other, unless a "defect" in their isolation temporarily brings about contacts, with the result that "matter" of differing dimensional space becomes interwoven. Only the absolute *Nothing*—which, as a thoroughly concrete *reality*, delimits the entire universe in ever-lasting rigidity, of hardness beyond earthly conception—is wholly devoid of space, outside of all potentially given space—absolute emptiness lacking all distance, to thinking minds incomprehensible even in forms of an image.

Eternal Space, however, permeates all worlds of differing spatial dimensions, without being likewise perceived—by virtue of their own conditioned perception of space—by those who experience themselves exclusively in those different worlds. Never could human beings experience *Eternal* Space if, in their timeless, innermost center of life, they were not *identical* with it in spiritual substance. This condition is not in the least affected by the majority's incapacity of becoming aware of themselves in this center during their mortal existence. However, this incapacity is not something one cannot escape, but simply a fateful result of complacent emotional lethargy. Needless to say, the intellect here will not be of help.

The intellect needs material to work with; and it seizes any material it is offered, starts working on it, and finally creates from it the best it can, depending on its own capacity and systematic schooling. Yet to find the innermost eternal core within oneself—the living spark of the Spirit's substance, which is able to carry the human consciousness into eternal existence, and there shall preserve it—to accomplish that there is need of different energies; but these, no less than the intellect, must be schooled and practiced, if during the time one still can physically use them, they are to contribute what lies in their power.

∾

CHAPTER TEN

ON INSIGHTS OF ASIAN RELIGIONS

M Y KNOWLEDGE OF ASIAN RELIGIOUS insights is truly not borrowed from books. Books always served only to reacquaint my mind with what had long before been familiar in spiritual ways. Yet I know that some Europeans, who derive their knowledge from books, are inclined to welcome ancient Eastern religious documents and prayer books as veritable psychological revelations, and to employ them as testimonials to bolster their own hypotheses. I also know, however, how much overvaluation lends weight to this judgment; and that, as a rule, such veneration is offered to distortions of erroneously, or merely partially understood religious speculations and notions of a distant early age no longer accessible to scrutiny. Nor, for that matter, is it obvious why it should reveal more wisdom when a mystical Asian text states the same ideas that, in the sphere of European culture, Meister Eckhart, Tauler, or the author of the *Theologia Germanica* formulated, or what Angelus Silesius, for instance, meant with the well-known verse,

"Heaven's bliss is in you, so are the pains of hell;
The choice is yours alone, and the reward as well."

There surely is no doubt, however, that the same truth reveals itself at times in completely new aspects when suddenly encountered in a formulation it has found in a far removed, unfamiliar cultural tradition. And herein finally lies also the chief practical significance of the texts from central Asian religious traditions. What constitutes the principal value of Eastern religious systems, which translation is able to convey, is not their particular *dogmas*, whose general aims have long been familiar, but rather the different form of expressing certain insights of entirely non-dogmatic nature; insights that had not been denied by any means likewise to ancient European religious culture; and this may lead to significant fresh approaches, and thus indeed prove the importance of the respective ancient Eastern religious writings made newly accessible.

It is characteristic that in the religious systems of Asia, risen or illuminated from the soil of India, the inner awakening of the Eternal is sought to be realized through a kind of inner drama of the soul, wherein the human being is at once actor and spectator. The individual's temperament thus represents its deities within itself and, subject to its nature, experiences them, with all the certainty of its own being, as alive and involved with itself—if not, indeed, attaining *subjective identity*, as shown for example in the case of Râmakrishna. The European temperament, by contrast, has pursued, even from ancient times, a form of religious quest, subject to its different nature, which is in fact the very opposite; namely, by seeking to experience *itself*—the human being—as alive in the Godhead. It is remarkable in this context that even Islam, which to us appears so obviously "Oriental," is part of this tradition. Christianity in particular, however, presents in all its forms, wherever it is lived with true conviction, precisely such religious experience of the primordial *Human* Being, veiled within the Godhead through the Godhead. Truly, an "anthropomorphism" that flesh and blood could not of itself have conveyed to the mortal creature shackled by earthly bondage.

Now it is possible to attain the experience of the Eternal either in the Asian or the European form. In both forms, however, this highest experience human beings are able to achieve during physical life on earth, is granted solely to those who are able to find their way through the thorny overgrowth of dogmas, which for centuries has been thriving like a thicket of wild roses, until at last they reach the innermost core of Truth: the lucid discernment of what the dogmas' creators had originally sought to protect, but thus, despite their best intentions, caused to be overgrown altogether. Apart from individual exceptions, of varying merit, however, Asians will do best, in objective recognition of their native endowment, to pursue the Asian, the European, by contrast, the European practice, wherever humans on earth seek to attain authentic experience of Eternity; for these two, so very different, approaches are psychophysically rooted, and not by any means simply "methods" randomly chosen at will. It is not possible either to combine the two approaches, nor can one change from one to the other, if the goal, common to both, is in truth to be reached.

Surely, no one will be in doubt for even a moment that what I teach is the European path to achieve the experience of timeless Reality. It is enriched, however, by everything that can be "acclimated" from Eastern sources of experience to the European form. Of course this does not contradict what has been said above concerning the impossibility of combining the two approaches, or to practice sometimes one, and then the other; for it would likewise be possible to make Asian teachings more fruitful by enriching them with insights of European experience. But even though, as a European, one comes to discover that, as one had remarked, in Asian texts the genuine fruits are at times "quite sparsely sown, and deeply hidden, while rigidly the negative lies everywhere at the surface," one must not let this experience mislead one to draw conclusions concerning the treasures that remain inaccessible to Europeans. Also Asians intending to search for traces of authentic experiences of eternal Reality in present-day

Europe would hardly find themselves in a different situation when examining Western religious writings.

What is often felt to be "demonic," however, is the indigenous, practical *occultism*, emerging in all religions of Asia; but this, for natives of the East, counts rather as an area of *physics*, which those acquainted with the field do not, in our sense, consider to be frightening. To the extent that such occult practice remains within the bounds of religion, the reins of religion will also still keep it in check; then even those who are spiritually far above the like regard it as harmless. Only where occultism itself becomes religion in Asia may it be judged "demonic" in the threatening sense.

One ought to approach the religious texts of the East with somewhat less awe, and more resolutely separate the chaff from the wheat; all the more so as the best, the most precious, most mysterious of all that Asia preserves has never become the subject of chronicles; and the few manuscripts from which it might be deduced will certainly never fall into the hands of any non-Asian.

❧

CHAPTER ELEVEN

ON THE
MYSTERY OF
THE ORIENT

WHEREVER DARKNESS IS ILLUMINATED BY a source of light, one will observe that also warmth is present near that source; but solely in the light's proximity, and not wherever by its rays it sheds illumination.

It thus is likewise the effect of the *Temple of Eternity*—an edifice of radiant spiritual substance, raised on a specific site on earth— and of the works performed in the domains of soul and Spirit, through the millennia, at that *Temple*'s site, that from this source of Light an unintended, but, given the nature of things, unavoidable spiritual influence will radiate throughout its geographical circumference; an influence that of necessity continues without ceasing. But since the site in question is situated amidst the highest mountains of the earth, and as these mountains constitute the vast tectonic geographical center of Asia, it is surely not surprising that from this site of the most intensive spiritual activity within this planet's sphere of life—although inaccessible to the material body—the constant vibrations here generated in the compact consistency of spiritual substance, continue to reverberate across considerable distances of that continent, until their effectiveness gradually fades.

It is to the power of these relatively far-reaching circles of radiant spiritual substance that the natives of Inner, East, and South Asia owe their soul's inclination to receive non-physical impressions within their consciousness; and therefore many an intuition reflecting Reality one would elsewhere look for in vain. This fact should not, of course, mislead one to conclude that every Asian traveler visiting the West will therefore automatically approach religious secrets with an open mind, let alone be in possession of enlightened spiritual insights. In all regions of Asia, no less than in Europe, and the other continents, there are tormented skeptics, mocking scoffers, lukewarm semi-believers, and, above all, legions who follow sundry superstitions; nor is it true, for that matter,

that only in Asia one finds superstition shoot-
ing like bamboo from the soil in the jungle.
But also in Asia there are, as everywhere else
in the world, profoundly reflective temperaments not content with all these things, who
feel the impulse to remove the inner isolation
that separates them from the conscious perception of the origin of their own lives and existence. That persons of such disposition have
been able, for thousands of years, to receive
the vibrations of spiritual substance, emanating from a point of the earth's surface, relatively close to them—as a related effect of the
spiritual transmissions of help and enlightenment, proceeding from there across the entire
world—accounts for the creation of that characteristic atmosphere embracing all things
spiritual—but likewise any number of pseudo-
spiritual phenomena—which to non-Asians,
who also seek the immutable in the ceaseless
change of all Being, appears so strange and
mysterious.

In our days this atmosphere, which had at one
time been able to draw into its orbit even the
originally alien faith of Islam, to the extent
that religion entered its geographically defin-
able, spiritually determined region—has lost

much of its radiant warmth. Not because its radiance has declined, but for the fact that non-Asian influences are spreading their corrosiveness within the circles of even the most gifted religious temperaments of Asia, and thus reduce the number of those able to maintain that imperturbable inner tranquility, which is the essential condition for discerning the radiant spiritual substance emanating from the site of the Spirit's *Temple of Eternity* on earth. Now as before, however, the appearance of so many concepts reflecting spiritual Reality, for which on other continents one would search in vain, is the result of the local proximity to the all-surpassing manifestations of eternal spiritual might, whose effects find expression in the souls of those gifted to feel them. In practice it does little harm that such expressions mostly are found in gardens of souls that foster colorful blooms of superstition; for in this way, superstition still serves as a positive element in creating temporal images reflecting timeless Reality.

Yet thoroughly mistaken would all non-Asians be who might get the idea they merely needed to catch the next boat, and then, from a port in India travel to Shimla or Darjeeling, and there would receive the radiance described in fullest abundance. Quite apart from the fact that even on Ceylon, on the islands of the Malaysian archipelago, in China, and Japan they certainly would not be beyond the range of this radiance, but could, instead, in all these locations infuse themselves with the choicest of auto-suggestions, without in the least suspecting it. But never could that come near their inner perception what even Asians, through countless generations prepared to that end in their nature, first must *learn* to perceive, in an apprenticeship lasting many years, in severity exceeding all Western conceptions; thus without mercy eradicating all sources of self-delusion. Even among Orientals only few have truly completed this schooling.

To attain the unfolding of latent organs of perception is certainly not as simple and easy as non-Asians like to imagine, after having just learned that self-development of this nature is possible. Only someone lacking all access to the kind of preparation that here is required could get the idea that attaining a capability permitting inner perception, for the sake of which countless lives are lived in the Orient

—for which every hardship is endured, each of the sometimes imposed self-punishments unconditionally suffered, bravely with pride —could also be achieved, almost without effort, by those not prepared, simply by an emotionally fostered receptiveness. The boundless arrogance that seriously believes the Orientals are making all these things unnecessarily difficult for themselves, as they naturally have no idea of the achievements of modern Western psychology, is here not worth further discussing. Such benighted conceit ranks far beneath even that vulgarized occultism that brazenly seeks to persuade its followers they could gain, from their innermost depth, everything that religious Orientals attain, and for which these dare risking their lives, simply by repeating, day after day, a series of faith-asserting claims that defy all facts of Reality.

It is very difficult, indeed, to come from the oldest cultural realms of the world and not be amused by Western civilization's fanciful superstitions, prone to be stretched in every direction.

ॐ

CHAPTER TWELVE

ON RELIGION
AND ITS FORMS

THE HUMAN BEING ON EARTH IS THE REQUIRED condition for the rise and the continued existence of religions in earthly life, but religions are not by any means the condition on which the earthly existence of human beings depends. This statement not merely follows from the well-known Gospel saying concerning the Jewish Sabbath (Mark 2:27), but is also, quite independently, a simple matter of logic no reasonable individual is likely to question. And yet there are legions of religious zealots, who, in defiance of all logic, would much prefer to turn this so explicit saying on its head. One can find them in all religions, although hardly anywhere in greater numbers than in precisely the religious denominations that claim to base themselves on the teachings of the sublime immortal who expressly called the Sabbath, and therewith all religious conventions, a purely *human affair*, "for the sake of man." Wherever the followers of any kind of religion forget the truth of this incontestable maxim, the respective form of religion provokes the imminent danger of losing its *religious* component, and thus to become an empty, petrified shell, whose principal purpose is then to secure its sterile existence, for the benefit of its servants, but at the cost of the flock that follows their lead. Instead of being a vessel *preserving* religion for the benefit, and in the service of human beings, the form becomes empty; and without mercy that emptiness, like a vacuum, swallows the human being, who ought to master the form through the content by humans created. One truly need not search for examples of this happening on earth today; for at this time it can be found everywhere.

But every form of religion that would not want to become an empty shell needs to take care that it will not grow *tolerant*, in that it exists solely on account of its *intolerance*, by excluding all other forms of religion. And every form of religion represents to its followers the exclusive path to *salvation*, even though this conviction is not explicitly voiced in its creed. This claim is self-evident, since all sincere followers of any religion want to see their temporal conduct justified, and their eternal salvation assured; and so they will certainly not give precedence to a form of religion of which they are not completely convinced that it deserves preference to all others, because in their view it alone will guide to salvation. The more tolerant the tone a form of religion seeks to adopt, the less it is able to preserve the essence of religion, the greater the danger of its becoming an empty shell, even if in name it continues to call itself a "religion."

Yet the intolerance every religion requires to justify its existence is a positive value only within the bounds of its own domain. The head of every household merely fulfills his rightful, traditional duty when he is intolerant of everything that might harm the household entrusted to his care. In the same way are those responsible for the continued existence of a religious convention entitled and justified, before their own conscience, to be intolerant, within the domain of their form of religion, of everything that might endanger the religious convention entrusted to their protection. However, beyond the bounds of this realm, which defines the specific nature of their form of religion, they lack every right and duty to exhibit intolerance. Only when the rights and duties of others, in the respective forms of religion entrusted to them, are strictly respected, without interference, is it possible to maintain the only level of reciprocal relationships that human dignity demands among the various forms of religion that, within their own domains, exclude each other's practice with justified intolerance; but coexistence of this kind remains the unconditional requirement allowing all to thrive. Any expansion of the intolerance required for its own existence, on its proper ground, beyond its rightful limits becomes an infringement of other forms of religion, which merely serves to support the hostility and ignorance confronting all forms of religion in this age, besieged by a thousand irritations, and grown weary of religious interference. Besides, the present age as a rule equates "religion" with mainly the "history of religion," which, as everyone familiar with the subject knows, presents examples of unwarranted transgressions of intolerance, warranted only internally, into the folds of other believers, which even the most implacable enmity toward religion could not imagine in ways more atrocious.

Above all, however, one should always bear in mind that religion in each of its forms, without exception, remains a purely mortal human surrogate, compassionately conceived in every instance by the eternal soul of individual human beings, out of concern for their fellow mortals, in order that even those not able to find it on their own might be offered a clear and well-marked path that will safely guide them to the realm that is eternal. It is foolish to debate which of these paths is less of a "detour"; for all alike are only such, as they would otherwise become too steep and perilous to serve the souls for whose benefit knowledgeable builders of such paths had once designed them. But I have not come to build yet another detour. Instead, I show the direct ascent into Light everlasting. This height, however, can be scaled only by souls that are able to summon sufficient inner energy, allowing them safely to leap across the abysses that others are taught to circumvent by way of a form of religion. My task is not to write an apologia for any particular form of religion or for many at once, although I surely could do so on firmer grounds than the professional apologists of religion. I must refer those in the bonds of a religion to the paths of their faith, and strive to find the daring souls who sought to reach Light by climbing their own paths, but went astray in their searching. I also must offer help to those who at one time had followed the well-marked paths of a form of religion, until, for one reason or another, they had lost confidence in the way prepared for them, and sought instead to pursue a different path across the wilderness of skepticism, but without making progress. Those making their way along the well-marked roads of their form of religion, satisfied and convinced of their cause, will certainly not find me blocking their way, even though at times I may be crossing their path. All I can do is to tell them, again and again, at the various turns in the road they do not understand, but are necessary, in which direction the ultimate goal of their quest is attained; and I bring them the spiritual strength to nourish their souls' weakening energy, to let them at least persevere on the path they have entered, until their souls are finally freed forever from their earthly encumbrance.

The notion of founding a "a new religion" is as far from my purpose as is offering existing religions any support other than the help accorded them by the eternal Spirit, on the strength of the timeless treasures they shelter. Wherever such help is needed, it neither requires one's asking, nor does it expect any thanks; and no efforts of earthly will could attain it.

❧

CHAPTER THIRTEEN

ON GIVING
CONSENT AND
THE POWER
OF FAITH

EACH FORM OF RELIGION THAT HAS gained a clear definition of its identity has every right to demand of its followers the honest consent to the teachings expressed in its self-definition, to the words of its founder or founders, and to its understanding of particular events it accepts as proven "historical" fact. This applies to the ancient indigenous religions of Asia, no less than to Buddhism in all its various forms, to the monotheism of the Pentateuch, to Christianity in its different denominations, as well as to Islam, the youngest of the great historically evolved religions. The consent to the respective formulations of the conceptual content presenting the unique property of a form of religion is regarded as the *belief* in this form of religion; and given that this consent rests upon the emotionally fostered assumption that the conceptual contents offered are true—an assumption regarded as "faith,"—one speaks of "confessions of faith." The inner consent, the self-imposed assumption that everything unfolded exactly as conveyed through the concepts that a given form of religion claims as its own "entrusted" heritage, is always the decisive factor of a person's recognized membership in a particular form of religion; and that remains unchanged, even though a form of religion may speak of itself as a "faith."

In the effort, certainly justified in principle, to sanction in one's proper domain only religious concepts supporting one's own convictions, and carefully to exclude everything alien and contradictory, one nearly everywhere had, through the centuries and millennia, so ominously overemphasized the importance of "confessions," that the formulation of the religious substance, for which consent is demanded by a given religion, over time gained more significance than the religious substance itself. Indeed, such consent—the willingness to regard something as true—proliferated into almost unbreakable shackles of the inner life of the different forms of religion. "Faith" in the form of merely assuming that something is true, mentally embraced and emotionally fathomed, has in nearly all religions to a large extent suffocated faith as a living energy, the highest power of the timeless soul. As a result, the assumed believers of a "faith," scarcely any longer know about that energy, so that one is likely to face complete lack of comprehension if one speaks of it to those who feel bound to a given religion.

This is not an inescapable "fate," however, but the consequence of lethargic indifference of the heart, which can, and must be, overcome, if the various forms of religion, created by human beings in the course of centuries and millennia, "for the sake of man,"—in order that every soul find itself where meaningful symbols may show it the way to reach inner Light—are not to turn into mere lifeless petrified shells.

Such petrifaction can effectively be prevented, however, only by the *living faith of the soul*; the *faith* that, from the inmost fire of the heart, will thirst for the self-revelation of its own life's ultimate Source in itself—no matter in which form of religion this is pursued, and however the concepts might be structured for which the soul's consent is required. This *faith* is not the assumed belief in the truth of any historical event or miraculous incident; it is no unquestioned acceptance of any transmitted teachings and opinions; but at the same time it is not in the least in conflict with all that is offered by a particular form of religion. Such *faith* has simply recognized that the events, conditionally or unconditionally assumed as "historical," no less than the transmitted teachings, for which its consent is required, are unavoidably needed by its form of religion to create the combinations of shapes and colors that are most clearly to *signify* for the soul the way to its inner Light; and this way is easy to follow for every soul devoted to its particular form of religion. On the way it is shown, *faith* then seeks with burning desire to apprehend the Source of its own life within it. It trusts innermost, incontestable feeling that one day, at the goal of its path, it shall encounter that Source of its being "face to face"; but even on the way toward that goal it already feels able to sense the energy that gives it life as a living presence within it, free of all anxiety of doubt. Imbued with such innermost *living faith*, the soul possesses itself in its center and is henceforth no longer in any danger of being able to content itself with simply mentally "believing" in the conceptual treasures of its earthly form of religion.

May the inner *faith*, having life through itself, once again be sought and found in every form of religion on earth by the souls that feel drawn to each, so that every realm of religious concepts may prove itself justified in its forms from within. But here it would be unforgivably foolish to think that I look upon one form of religion or another with sympathy, but were able to disrespect others. Instead, I know where *in all of them* one can find the one thing that needs to be found; and I seek to make readers recognize how it practically is attainable in every form of religion, even though each is compelled, on its own account, to deny its attainment to all other forms of religion, as it otherwise could justify its own existence only to those having gained spiritual knowledge. Nor is there any need with every means to campaign against the claim of universal exclusivity, a given form of religion believes to possess before others. All by itself will such a foolishly hopeless claim again and again be confined to its limits, in any age that has to confront it.

&

CHAPTER FOURTEEN

ON MISTAKEN
IMAGES OF GOD

HOWEVER LOFTY THE HEIGHTS MAY BE TO which human beings elevate themselves in their thinking, they always will, without intending to, transform themselves into *images* and *symbols*; and in the same way their thinking converts other things into *images* and *symbols*. Even Muslims cannot do without image and likeness in their conceptual spheres, despite the fact that Islam, according to strict, though questionable interpretation, forbids depicting the human figure. Fortunately, this has not prevented that in Persian and Indian cultural regions of Islam there had once been created the most splendid miniatures, depicting human beings full of passion and fiery vitality, without giving offense to pious souls at that time in those lands. In other forms of religion, which did not feel it necessary to fear the peril of being magically overwhelmed by visual depictions of humans, the representation of the human form has been elevated, as every informed person knows, to the highest potential of art; for here such representation wanted to serve as a sermon, striving for the highest intensity of persuasion, which the eye is at all times able to exert on the soul. Nor could the conceptual domains of the various forms of religion ever dispense with image and symbol when representing the human being in *language*; for thus it entered the souls of the listeners, and thereby became their own. In this way to place a transparent, visually concrete image in front of the spiritual Reality, which humans could otherwise not apprehend, may surely, at the very highest levels of the soul, also lead to sublime empathy, and thus to knowledge of God in the light of eternal love. More commonly, however, human mortals are inclined to give that self-created image, placed before their inner vision, ever more compact shape; yet in this way, they also strive to mold it into something closely resembling earthly models.

Wherever the aim was forming a concept of God—the primordial Self-Generation to which all things created owe existence and life—humans on earth have at all times tragically found themselves urged to seek their models among their own kind, where such surpassed them in temporal power. Thus, in the conceptual realm of humans, "God" has become a "king" of an eternal "kingdom"; and the soul, which in truth seeks to experience eternal Reality, instead remains trapped in the billowing folds of a quite robust representation of human craving to wield power on earth. It is practically impossible to construe a concept of God that could be yet farther removed from God's timeless Reality. Nonetheless, it is according to this general earthly model that the conceptual images of God have been shaped by the greatest religions that human beings on earth have been able to create for themselves.

Even though millions may seek to worship these conceptual images with all the love and fervor of their souls, while other millions serve them only from fear of the power their own belief assumes they possess, one also should not be surprised to see the numbers of those constantly growing, who finally were able to overcome their instinctive fear, or who one day saw their fervent love extinguished by bitter disenchantment, so that they now dismiss all images of God as constructs of human delusion, simply because they recognized their own as unreal. Those obstruct their way most thoroughly who have been dis-enchanted: who rid themselves of their enchantment. In their resentment at having been able to deceive themselves, they overlook that their deception was merely the effect of a conceptual image; and so they now assume that Reality has been exposed as being unreal, simply because a faulty image of it has collapsed.

It serves no purpose to accuse the disenchanted of having "no faith"; but it is necessary to show them how they, within themselves, may grow aware of what truly is *real*, which they in vain had sought to approach from without, through a conceptual image that now lies demolished before them. In order to show, through instruction, how one is granted within oneself to experience Reality—as the primordial Source of one's own timeless being—conceptual images shall certainly also be needed; yet these images will carefully avoid any physical likeness that is not most lucidly transparent. And everything that may be conveyed in figurative words shall serve no other goal than to awaken in those being instructed the conceptual image of the *structure* of timeless Reality, wherein and through which they themselves are given their lives. God is such a multitude of many-sided things of infinite diversity and difference, at both the selfsame Time and Eternity, that it would never be possible to convey what God truly is, unless one could in broad general outline describe the *structure* of the *Spirit's Life*, whose consciousness of Self is God. The aspects of God's Being I outlined in this way, proceeding from the spiritually effective numerical value of ONE, through the various values up to the number of TWELVE—which the human mind can only envision as separate, intermediate levels—are exclusively meant to be understood in that sense. Yet here one must not think at any stage of levels that are one above, or next to one another, which is the only way possible in physical life. Instead, one should try intuitively to sense a seamless, equally timeless One-within-the-Other, because it is not possible mentally to evoke an image of this Being-One-Self, whose aspects are mutually imbuing each other in the Spirit's structure.

Nor is it my intention to suggest a concept where I am able to convey *Reality itself* to the intuitive perception of my fellow mortals. How close this eternal Reality has come to them in my words, some will fathom, others consciously experience, as long as these words shall reach human beings.

CHAPTER FIFTEEN

ON THE INTENT
OF ALL TEACHING

I N ALL THE INFINITELY DIFFERENTIATED Self-manifestations of God within the structure of Life in the timeless Spirit, God remains —in every self-willed form revealing God— consciousness of absolute eternal Self.

In the same way, the actual ultimate goal of human beings on earth in all their intentions and actions, their will to exist and to manifest form, is in reality, *self-affirmation* of the God-engendered energies of their eternal soul within the conscious self of their own being; for only in thus being conscious of *self* can the soul once again enter, and awaken in God. Only through self-affirmation by one's self being conscious in the consciousness of God's Self is union of love with God in God possible. Until then the soul is merely in *expectation* of love; and what it takes for its "love" of

God is no more than longing for love, in that it offers the fervor of its love to a power above it, in which to "believe" it may well be admonished, but of whose nature it truly knows nothing. For only in the individual soul, which in each case unifies them all in forever lasting union, can the timeless energies of the soul once more regain their self-consciousness within the Eternal, from where they went forth, to be absorbed again by their Origin, in a self-given form—crystallized around an eternal core of spiritual consciousness, imbuing all with its light, and lending its own individual color to all that form part of that core's luminous essence.

Yet what is here described is not merely something that thought may envision, but an event objectively unfolding in Reality; and everything being taught serves exclusively to let this event take place in the soul, by removing, as far as is possible, all erroneous concepts that obstruct its occurring, and to make room instead for concepts that effectively prepare its experience.

For that reason, everything necessity constrains me to say about the One and infinitely

Manifold that "God" comprises has not been stated to be intellectually dissected, but rather to reawaken in the soul those concepts which it still unconsciously retains in itself from the eternal Origin of its own timeless energies. What I state expects no readiness to "believe," nor does it want to be "understood." It seeks instead to make conscious again in the soul's timeless energies the memory that corresponds with that Origin. Yet this will succeed the sooner, the more the reader controls the mind's speculative thinking, which treats my words as little more than material for playing mental games. At issue here is an actual *transformation* of the soul's state of *consciousness*, not merely a different way of "thinking." Only this very profound transformation of its consciousness, which normally is held to be immutable in life on earth, informs the soul with the incontrovertible *certainty*, which it forever strives in vain to find by intellectual efforts. Eternal Reality is unattainable by virtue of mental deductions. Consciousness alone is able to *sense* it, and only by *sensing* it does it grant confirmation. This confirmation is so perfect, however, that there remains not even the faintest desire mentally to comprehend what has been attained.

To make it possible to awaken this inner experience, I have in every instance chosen words that convey it. These must not be mingled with others of seemingly similar meaning. On the other hand, one should not make a cult of them, nor scour them painstakingly for secret meanings. Instead, one ought to receive them in lucid simplicity, seeking to let the soul apprehend them as they are given. But one must never make them the basis or start for one's own intellectual speculations. Again, I care little for mental "consent"; and nothing could be farther from my aim than seeking to "convince" through persuasion. I call upon readers to put my words to the test by applying them in practice. But in order to test them in practice, they need to be consciously *felt*, until, as emotional experience, they become the private possession of those who receive them. First and foremost, my words are designed to *contain*, to *transmit*, and to *awaken* inner experience. What their "meaning" provides in addition is only of secondary importance, though it certainly may also help to admonish the soul to accept what it is offered as experience it thus may possess. Even in regard to their "meaning," my words are primarily to be received as means to awaken such inner experience.

❧

CHAPTER SIXTEEN

WHERE I AM BUT THE MESSENGER

I T IS NEITHER MY SPIRITUALLY GIVEN temporal task, nor my earthly human, wish-induced intention, let alone my personal will, to prophesy events that may, or must and, therefore, shall occur in time to come.

I have never understood, nor even been able to feel others' desire to know in advance what the future will bring; and I would find it an intolerable burden were I intended to guard knowledge of coming external events within me, or worse, had to predict them in public.

If nonetheless there are passages in my writings—in *The Book on the Living God*, in *The Book on Human Nature*, in the guidance on social ethics, *The Mirage of True Freedom*, and above all in *The Book on Love*—which refer to future possibilities in the realm of earthly human affairs, then what is stated here presents something substantially more significant than any prediction of future external earthly events would ever be able to offer.

In all those passages—without exception—I was not prompted by any sort of "foreknowledge" of particular earthly events to set down what I put into writing, but was bound by spiritual duty to express, in words of my native tongue, what I was granted to take with me from my spiritual Ground of primordial Being.

Such spiritual obligation does not by any means, however, at the same time impart the earthly mental knowledge about the particular dates, persons, and places involved in things spiritually disclosed; nor about the circumstances leading to the events I was obliged to make known. In other words, wherever in my writings there are references to future events on earth, I am no more than the messenger of purely spiritual tidings I was made to deliver, but in no position to offer commentaries on what has been stated. May all readers interpret in their own ways what I merely transmit in words, should they feel it necessary. Concerning this, I enjoy no advantage over them; but I also have no right to offer the public a personal interpretation of such passages, nor even to express the like to those who are closest to me in life on earth.

Where, as spiritual Mediator, it is my task in words to transmit what I received, I know only that, and why, the content presents absolute, incontrovertible *certainty*; and I would be compelled to convey it, even if I myself were deprived of any chance to interpret what I alone was to recognize. Where, on the other hand, I take from *my own* within the eternal Spirit what I am able to make known and to offer, one shall most certainly never find me predicting future events; unless one here should include life "after death," which indeed still lies in the future of my readers, but to me is a state of continuous presence, together with the simultaneous physical life on earth.

I certainly do not deny, however, that out of my own in the timeless Spirit I am conscious also of things that lie in the future, as well as of those far in the past, no less than of that which in earthly time is still presence. But thus being conscious means to experience again what long ago had been felt by human souls in their lives on earth; it compels one to share what in present physical time souls are exposed to, owing to earthly determined experience; and it lets one partake in advance of what only future events will cause to be felt in the realm of the soul. At no point of thus taking part in what is felt and experienced am I at the same time also conscious, nor even in image aware, of the external circumstances that once had physically caused, are presently causing, or shall in future bring forth what is endured by my soul. In that respect, I myself determine precisely the limits of the experiences I share; and these limits I guard against everything I am not compelled to endure, but which nonetheless seeks to force its way into my consciousness. But what I am bound to accept, feel, and experience, due to my purely spiritually governed commitment, is likewise intended for only my personal insight, and is never to become material for any prediction, even where it includes future events.

The reason, however, for which it was at various times made my task—through the consciousness and will of the One, in whom I am eternally born in the Spirit—to transmit remarks concerning the future, will become clear only to future generations. Before confirmation has proved what my words must situate in a future I am myself unable to measure in physical terms, no one can recognize what only later generations will discern in the proof they are offered.

❧

CHAPTER SEVENTEEN

TO WHOM I HAVE
NOTHING TO SAY

E VERYTHING THAT I HAVE COME TO SAY HAS only been said to call those for whom it is meant toward their conscious awakening in the timeless Light of the Spirit, whose substance is the primordial Ground of their being, and as such the only certainty of life everlasting. I do not want to awaken those, however, who still are in need of their sleep. To them I have nothing to say; and what they nonetheless hear when I speak to those I know as my own, remains to them only a jumble of sounds, heard by the ear of a sleeper, which cannot make sense of what it received. They still are dreaming with open eyes; and the world of their dreams is their only conscious "reality." One must let those deluded by their dreams continue sleeping, until they shall themselves grow tired of their sleep; be it still in earthly life, or only after they no longer can obtain the help their earthly body could have offered them. The "night when no one is able to work" is "night" for only those who did not strive to use the spiritual resources of their earthly body; and of them alone is it said that "no one" is able to "work" in the darkness of night. It surely is not easy to see through one's dreams in bright daylight, and to recognize that the reality one is dreaming is "real" only for the dream in which it is thought to be such. It is infinitely easier, however, to come to this recognition while the mortal body still can provide the physical resonance for discerning what in fact is truly Eternal, than that is possible after the temporal body's death, which terminates this potential forever.

Those one must not disturb in their dreams, as they will not yet tire of sleeping for some time to come, are naturally far from perceiving these things; nor do they want to know anything likely to wake them up. They feel far too comfortable in their dreaming, to which they give the name of "lucid thinking," to be able to feel even the slightest desire to exchange their condition for any other. In the belief that all darkness must give way to the clarity of their probing mind, they suspect only error and delusion wherever their dream-life's probing fails to shed light, given that only the soul's awakened faculty of perception is able to sense the eternal Spirit's radiant substance. And none of those feeling so sure of themselves in their dreams grows aware of the importance their physical body could have for them, if they were able to put it to use as a tool, offered them for a time, to intensify sensations felt, and thus making it immeasurably easier for the soul to draw more closely to the consciousness of the physical mind what in the Spirit was fathomed as barely a breath.

To all of those so sure of themselves and of their views, I have nothing to say; and what I say is not intended for them. Not until their absolute certainty one day becomes suspect even to them will they find their way to me; and only then will I have something to say also to them.

But never shall I have anything to say to those, who, like burrowing rodents, gnaw at the roots of all secrets that to know from within they have not been called. They are no less merely dreaming with open eyes, like the others; only their dreaming indulges a taste for unsavory greed, and hidden craving for power over forces that, for good cause, are far above their reach. Even though, in witless presumption, the minds of such looters were to take whatever I have to say to others as if it were meant for them, they still could never make it their own; for what I have to say needs to be felt in one's depth. Those who hunger after secret powers, however, would cunningly pry into things of which I tell others that one cannot experience them but *from within*.

All who truly would count among those to whom I have something to say must not indulge the illusion that I intend to bring them the type of "knowledge," they simply may add to their earthly learning acquired before, and thus will likewise possess. They will not actually grasp what I have to convey to them until in every word they feel nothing but my will to awaken their soul's own *sensibility*; and only then will my words indeed have something to say to them. Everything I say wants to be *felt*; it is not given with the idea of presenting the intellectual acuity of readers an exercise to practice their mental skills of analysis.

And so I also have nothing to say to any of those who busily seek to adjust what they heard from me to other things received somewhere else; for what I give is distorted at once if one interprets my words as if they sought to lend support to any philosophical or creed-determined system of thinking. What I say bears testimony to the Spirit's timeless Reality; and it has become word solely through that Reality's Self-experience. What I offer may be compared to carefully drawn maps, which protect the traveler from going astray. But those seeking to know the country itself will benefit little from merely "knowing" about the roads. Only by actually entering them will their sensibility apprehend what until then had been concealed.

❧

CHAPTER EIGHTEEN

ON THE SOUL'S ETERNAL SALVATION

I F IT IS SAID, AGAIN AND AGAIN, THAT THE PATH to eternal Light, indeed, the realm of eternal Light itself—from which the indestructible core of spiritual human existence, the timeless scintilla of the Spirit's substance, proceeds, and to which that scintilla must once more return, *with or without* the human mortal's individuated consciousness—if it is said that this path can only be found *within*, this admonition most certainly does not imply that the earth-born human nature encloses within itself the realm of eternal spiritual Light, and the path to its realm, in the way that a vessel encloses its contents. In reality, the human being of this earth is, instead, a combination of a group of highly dissimilar realms of perceptive faculties; and the path toward Light leads from one of these realms to the next, ever closer to the innermost region. From most ancient times, to be sure, have all who knew of this path described it in the image of an ascent, and of a sequence of steps; yet here one must not think of a path that leads to a goal in the distance, but never lose sight of the fact that each ascending "step" on the "path" to Light represents a step toward the *inner self*, and is *higher* than the preceding one only in being farther *within*. The path consists of concentric regions of increasingly luminous sensibility. One could try to present it also through a technical model, by placing a sizable number of variously colored panes of glass in front of a source of light, so that each of these panes could be removed in succession. At first hardly a glimmer would penetrate all these panes; but the more one would remove of the outermost, which would also have to be of the darkest color, the more distinctly would the form of the light burning within become apparent to the eye, even though still observed through various colors, until the innermost, entirely color-free pane at last would also reveal the Light's own true color in purity.

In accord with their animal nature, born into in the external physical world, known to all, human beings regard it as their first, most obvious, not seldom even their only task, to be conscious of, and to explore, merely the outermost realm of sensibility, which extends to little more than their animal psyche. Yet despite the almost impenetrable density of the external sphere of sensibility, the only region known to them, human beings time and again became aware of inner Light, feeling its presence within them, even though it was able to dawn in them only as a faint intuition. In this way human beings discovered that also other realms of sensibility were given them, through which they could more closely approach the Light discerned through intuition; and even if, as a rule, they only reached the domain of images, as given form in the revelations of their respective religions, this nonetheless proved a significant step; for to this level all could be guided, and thus made aware, at least by virtue of images, of their innermost nature.

Many, however, are capable of attaining more; although among these not all are able to

muster the confident strength, demanded unconditionally for many years, if not decades,
before entering those domains of sensibility
in which the energies of the soul can be experienced directly; or will find their way into the
innermost realm, wherein exclusively the
timeless scintilla of the Spirit, around which
the eternal soul's energies *crystallize*, bestows
itself on the conscious perception of human
mortals on earth. But just as in external physical life many significant, and for the future
ground-breaking things, can by no means be
experienced or comprehended by everyone,
even though the effects of these things are felt
by all of humanity, excluding only those who
exclude themselves, so it is likewise sufficient to learn about things in the Spirit's domain not everyone can experience and
mentally grasp, through the disclosures of the
Luminaries of primordial Light—who alone
are capable of experience in the dimensions
concerned, and throughout the millennia continue to find their Mediator—if the danger is
to be avoided that human beings shall exclude themselves by force of misdirected will.
The "salvation of the soul" is determined by a
person's *will*, not by assuming that certain

narratives and teachings of creed are "true."
Once the will of human mortals refuses to
receive its directives in future exclusively
from its animal psyche, then by this resolve
alone do such individuals place themselves
under the guidance of the eternal spiritual
scintilla, which lives its life within them,
whereby their own eternal soul is gradually
given the form that it needs, so that it can
accept the human being's otherwise impermanent temporal consciousness into its own
unchangeable permanence. This *transfusion*
proceeds without in the least being noted, and
independent of which inner regions of sensibility a mortal human being may already have
attained. Nothing but a human being's own
volition can separate again what has been
integrated in this way.

❧

CHAPTER NINETEEN

HOW THE URGE TO ASK QUESTIONS DELAYS ONE'S ADVANCE

WHEN AN ANSWER RECEIVED GIVES RISE to another question, this most obviously proves that the answer has not been absorbed and made truly one's own. How often do I still have to repeat that it clearly is not my task to supply the mortal mind's luxuriously proliferating urge to ask questions with needless inspiration for additional inquiries? Far more than obligation required I patiently went out of my way to accommodate the human urge to ask questions, but one surely cannot claim that in so doing I have omitted repeatedly to point out how worthless is all desire for knowledge that wastes itself in asking questions, and how useless every answer that does not lead to finding it oneself. Even if one knew everything the wisest of all ages had ever taught or written down in the languages of their people concerning the primordial Ground of human spiritual life, one thereby would not have come one hair's breadth closer to the primordial Ground of one's own spiritual life. By contrast, one is able inwardly to grow aware of it without having read one word of those sages, or knowing anything of all that could be said about the timeless primordial Ground of human spiritual life.

Giving in to the urge to ask questions leads every time to a considerable weakening of one's inner sensibility; it demonstrates willingness to attempt, with inappropriate means, perhaps more quickly to gain insights that can be attained solely through awakened sensibility, but only after an appointed period of time. The desire for answers from external sources displays a readiness to settle for a mentally comprehensible representation of what should in fact become one's own in its complete reality, but which is discernible as such only to one's sensibility. Those who feel their keen intelligence is duly featured before themselves and others by asking ever new questions, delude merely themselves, because they seek a definitive decision that can never be made where they so confidently expect it. They are like someone taking off in an airplane, attempting to catch fish—in the clouds. The questions that are truly justified on the path toward Light and enlightenment cannot be put into words; they solely gain form in one's sensibility, and only there they also are given their answer. All questions in words, by contrast, merely delay receiving the answer discerned in the soul itself. After all, at issue here is not a topic that may adequately be expressed in words, even if the most miraculous vocabulary were to offer itself for the purpose. Nor is the goal to be attained something that is such as it is, but could just as well be a different way, even though it may be described in infinitely varied forms. The quest here instead is solely the hidden primordial Ground of Being, manifest as radiant substance, both within one's temporal existence, and also one's enduring life within the timeless Spirit's essence.

But the day when mortal human beings have even once experienced, through their body's senses, the primordial Ground of their own life—which continuously manifests itself throughout all generations, with individuated form endowing every single being—then only will the recognition of their former folly make them shudder at the notion that this First and Last, at once Unique and Infinitely Manifold, would let itself be found by asking questions, or could be made to answer questioning words. After all, no verbal disclosures concerning the inner connections of life in the Spirit's radiant substance can ever replace one's own becoming conscious within; nor can any presentation based upon thought ever bestow the certainty that is brought about in one's bodily sensed awareness solely by the conscious inner perception of the One giving life in Itself to infinities without number. The sphere of all questions has here reached its end; and every mentally driven impulse of asking dissolves. But even though entering this innermost region of sensibility is granted to only few, since but the smallest number know how to wait for it; lucid insight nonetheless remains open to all, wherever their sensibility seeks to include itself within the Eternal: refraining without questions from every mentally prompted urge to keep asking, but instead being turned toward Reality, which can reveal itself solely to consciousness of awakened sensibility.

❦

CHAPTER TWENTY

ON THE TIMELESS AND TEMPORAL FORM OF THE SOUL

F OR HUMAN BEINGS TO DENY THAT ANIMALS have a soul appears inconceivably foolish; but it also becomes seemingly incomprehensible, given the certainty that by far the majority of human mortals knows nothing other than precisely that animal soul as their own "soul," and are scarcely, or not at all, capable of discerning within them the timeless soul, formed of eternal energies, and thus, owing to their substance, abiding in permanence without end. Even so, however, this error is quite understandable, in that human beings consider everything supra-physical in themselves— which, like the animal soul, is merely the functional effect of the life of the cells in their visible, animal-related body—as belonging to their eternal soul, of whose existence they had been told by those of their kind who were able to experience themselves in its realm. That observation nonetheless led humans to discover in animals something similar to what in themselves seemed to belong to the eternal soul, is clearly shown by the frequently recurring fairy tale motif in which animals appear, which are in truth human beings in animal disguise, or humans magically turned into animals by the power of wicked sorcerers. Humans felt it was eerie having to observe that animals, which, according to most religious creeds, could *not* have a "soul," nonetheless displayed traces of such; and where religious faith accepted reincarnation, the concept that human souls might find themselves fettered within animals, surely encountered no excluding resistance—given the belief in metempsychosis itself merely resulted from the recognition of similar traits and behavior found among humans and animals.

As I have briefly set forth in the short chapter "En soph" in *The Book on the Living God*, the Night of primordial Being, in constant tremors shaking its cosmic rigidity, expels without ceasing dark energies—sparks, as it were, of its own eternally inexhaustible substance—

timeless primordial Being, like Itself, which, having completed what they were to effect in a given cycle of creation, once more return to their source. In that context I explained how these energies of primordial Being are the cause of all generation of form throughout the universe. I also showed, however, that their effects are manifest in very different forms. One of the most rarified of these energies I described as being those that radiate in absolute clarity in the primordial Light, which bestow form on the individuated, timeless soul of the human being. The attainment of this form can only come about, however, if the eternal scintilla of the Spirit—being the source of permanent individuation in the Spirit, and also the cause of all individuation in temporal life—is able to crystallize those energies of the soul around itself, by virtue of the human being's will to submit them for unification by the Spirit's scintilla. Like everything that has been given form, also the animal component of mortal human beings, including their will, is merely the consequence effected by those ju into the Night of Primordial Being, after having completed the respective cycle of their effectiveness. In regard to the animal, this

completion is accomplished with the for-
mation of the *animal soul*, which, just as in
mortal human beings—to the extent their animal nature is concerned—shows itself merely
as the temporal function resulting from the
animal's given organism, and therefore ceases
to exist, as soon as that organism is no longer
able to fulfill what its life requires. The decisive difference between animals and human
beings on earth consists in the fact that human
beings, even in their bondage to the animal,
in which they are chained on earth, retain the
freedom to grow conscious of themselves as
being eternal scintillas of the Spirit, born of
primordial Light; and this again is only possible in physical existence because human
beings on earth are not merely the consequence effected by energies of primordial
Being that are able to generate forms only in
the physical domain, but find within themselves, in direct relationship, as their own
possession, those sublime primordial energies
that Light is able to illuminate; energies,
which purely through their own eternal permanence and substance vouchsafe immortal-
ity to the soul of the human being. It is the
necessary, liberating task of human beings,
self-chosen through their physical existence,

to *unify*, in the crystallizing center of their eternal essence, the highest form of the primordial energies of Being—which, as primordial Being gain radiance in primordial Light, thus forming the energies of their soul, in order finally to serve, within the primordial Word, the timeless form of the soul. That is brought about, however, by a constant act of a human being's temporal will, which, as pointed out, is but the consequence effected by those primitive forms of the eternal energies of primordial Being, whose highest form, accessible to mortal human beings, is that which constitutes the energies of their eternal soul.

All sensibility of things eternal is made possible for human beings, having *fallen into* existence on earth, only through the eternal energies of the soul—but not unless they have found their lord and master in the Spirit's timeless *scintilla* of the human being, and thus achieved their *unification*. However mysterious and sublime all energies of the eternal soul are in themselves, each nonetheless asserts its own exclusive will, and if not gathered in an individually determined soul, will merely manifest itself, and its own given impulse. As a result, the human being's earthly nature, despite the wealth of energies that form its soul, may still be lost to the human's spiritual consciousness, unless the individual *constantly* strives, as best as earthly encumbrance will allow, to align its temporal, *secondary* will, which is merely the consequent effect of the Spirit's primordial Being, with the *primary* will of its eternal spiritual scintilla. For solely in this *eternity-oriented* will can the timeless energies of the soul be united, according to spiritually given formations, in the eternally abiding human soul. And only in this way will also be reached that festive attainment of *union*, whereby the human being's purely physical consciousness receives the fruit-bearing infusion from the Spirit's eternal hierarchical realm of human individuation, by embracing its own scintilla of the Spirit within itself. Having accomplished that, the henceforth spiritually illuminated individual shall then experience the *birth* of the *Living God* in its own, individually formed timeless soul.

⚬₰

CHAPTER TWENTY-ONE

WHAT SURVIVES
AFTER DEATH

I T CERTAINLY WOULD BE CORRECT TO ASSUME that after the human body's death, the animal soul of the human being—including everything at any time experienced within it, as having been merely the functional effect of a body, which now can no longer perform any such function—must cease to exist, as is the case with every animal, which also loses its soul after death. Indeed, this assumption would be correct, were it not for the fact that during the bodily life of human beings the animal soul had undergone such an intensive union of sensibility with the enduring eternal soul that the impressions experienced by the animal soul find themselves interwoven in countless ways with the energies of the soul that survives. Yet even though after the death of the human being the animal soul as such can no longer exist, whatever had been experienced within it until its final extinction is preserved, for the time being, with and among the eternal soul's own wealth of experience; and, using human standards of measuring time, it may take decades, centuries, millennia, and longer—depending on the nature of the experience, and the intensity of its impression—before the final selection can be effected by the will of the timeless soul; this choice will determine which memories the eternal consciousness retains as continuous *presence*, and those which the timeless soul will let be extinguished forever. The soul's eternal energies, whose countless multitudes constitute the human being's timeless soul during life on earth, giving it form by virtue of human will and action, have shared the feelings and experiences that once had been felt and known by the animal soul, and they retain it in the timeless soul's consciousness, until the latter, by an act of its will, decides what is to remain its own, and what instead is to vanish.

To make this decision immediately after the death of the physical body is impossible, because the various experiences rooted in the animal soul have been imprinted upon the eternal soul's energies in greatly varying intensity, depending on the specific impulses that had caused the animal soul's sensibility simultaneously to bring about corresponding vibrations also in the energies of the timeless soul. The latter, however, cannot freely decide what it intends to retain in its permanent consciousness, or would see expelled from it, until all the impulses have been exhausted through which at one time a sensation felt by the animal soul was able to impress itself on the timeless soul's energies. All consciousness of *identity*, however, is contained exclusively in those combinations of sensibility which the eternal soul shall one day wish to become a permanent part of itself. What it expels, by contrast, is thereby extinguished forever; just as, at the death of an animal, everything dissolves that had ever become conscious experience in the animal's soul. For out of all things the animal experienced only that can become permanent what impressed the eternal soul's energies of a human being, who shared the animal's experience, as a *human emotion*, thus leaving impressions as memories, retained as enduring presence. By contrast, the dark primordial energies of Being,

devoid of individuated consciousness, which
had been the cause of the animal's life, bodily
form, and soul, were affected only indirectly
by the animal's experience, insofar as an intensive, and long repeatedly sensed impression in the animal soul, is able to condition,
as it were, the various primordial energies, so
that in their next, instinctively sought forma-
tion the impulses might assert themselves
which in the preceding combination those
energies had received. The same is true of the
mortal human being, concerning its animal
life, animal body, and animal soul.

When it is said that the soul might *suffer
harm*, and thereby one means the eternal soul,
this statement refers to, and ought to be
understood in a purely figurative sense; for in
reality the eternal soul can never be harmed,
let alone suffer death through anything physical. However, it most certainly can be lost to
the human mortal—even as the human mortal may be lost to the soul—so that everything
that once had been given spiritual life in
physical time, by virtue of the soul's eternal
energies, is fated to die in the human being.
As for the human being's animal soul, however, the latter may truly offer the timeless

human soul memories of enduring *presence*, which the eternal soul would want to preserve for itself, even when the impulses, which once had impressed themselves on that soul, have long ago been exhausted. In this way, the *identity* of consciousness, unifying the human being that once had lived its life on earth, with that being's timeless soul, shall be attained for all eternity. With no less effectiveness, however, the eternal soul may equally be burdened, by the animal soul's instincts, with things inherently alien to its nature, thereby precluding, for immeasurable periods of time, any unification of the former temporal with the eternal consciousness, or making this unification impossible for eternity.

As for the gifts their timeless soul may grant them, human beings need truly not feel apprehensive. On the other hand, during their life on earth they can hardly be watchful enough to assure that their animal soul will offer what their eternal soul is able to preserve forever.

෴

CHAPTER TWENTY-TWO

ON A NAME
AND A MERE
EXPEDIENT

I F WHAT IS MERELY A FUNCTIONAL EFFECT OF the animal body's organism, brought about and physically perceptible on earth for only a limited time, is referred to as "soul," in that one speaks of the *animal soul*, and the same word is used to denote that physically imperceptible timeless reality—which is the permanent world wherein the individuated, eternal spiritual scintilla finds its expression—such use of the same word to designate both is here fully justified. Although the *animal soul* is merely an *indirect* result effected by primordial energies at their lowest, darkest level of instincts and drives, where the myriads of such energies taking part in the life of an organism are devoid of self-consciousness—while the *eternal soul* lets its form be created by many thousands of fully conscious primordial energies, radiant in primordial Light, at the highest level human beings can apprehend, and as such represents a *direct* manifestation of the sublime energies of primordial Being—both forms nonetheless are very similar in the way they are known through experience. Using the same name for both thus characterizes merely the similar form in which the two are experienced. The very fact that both these domains of sense perception and experience must let their similarity be signified by the same name, which is a different word in every language, clearly suggests that the name "soul" does not represent a phonetic rendition based on a particular sequence of letters, but instead is meant as a *descriptive name* for something that truly exists, but cannot be seen by physical eyes.

By contrast, the definition of the earthly human being as a visible mortal body and an immortal soul is merely an expedient to which human minds, living in bondage to earthly existence resorted after becoming aware that something other than merely their body's visible nature expressed itself in the human being. Such an expedient definition was sufficient in times of credulous acceptance of primitive explanations of all things that physical senses perceived. It is no longer adequate, however, now that humans on earth have begun to feel the need critically to compare their observations. As a result, the retention of this mental expedient was bound to increasingly weaken the ability to sense the eternal soul, after critical observation grew steadily more aware of the *animal soul*, and was forced to recognize that here one was dealing with nothing more than the temporal effect of the functions of the impermanent earthly life, due to animal energies, even if far superior to the animal's level. The more the sensibility of human beings now was concentrated on the *animal soul*, which in reality truly exists for a time, but then is bound to dissolve, the less could their sensibility remain capable also of feeling the eternal soul. This incapacity remains the same whether one considered what had been sensed—not altogether mistakenly—as proof that every observed activity of the soul had to be attributed solely to the physical body, or whether, on the contrary, one regarded everything that in truth had its cause exclusively in the *animal soul*, already as a manifestation of the *eternal soul.* Both errors can be avoided only if one knows that in all activities of the soul that humans on earth experience one is facing two dimensions of life that need to be clearly differentiated, but which are similar in respect to their manifestations.

To be sure, for those who are not fully conscious in spiritual life it is practically impossible to determine in every individual case which inner manifestations are still the effect of the *animal soul*, and which without question confirm the existence of the everlasting immortal soul. Both are too closely interwoven with each other to make that distinction. Nonetheless, there is a significant difference, given that everything felt and experienced in the animal soul also reaches the consciousness of the eternal soul; indeed is preserved in the latter, while it requires careful attuning of the animal soul, and years of patient constancy, if it is to gain so much as only the certainty that the enduring soul truly exists. This does not hinder the human animal soul, however, from continuously receiving influences due to the eternal soul, without being aware of the latter's origin and nature. It is thanks to these influences that the animal soul of human beings is able to rise immeasurable heights above the souls of the other creatures on earth—as this may be seen in the realm of the creative arts—although it remains equally possible that humans reach barely the degree of development of their animal soul that often is found even in higher species of animals.

❧

CHAPTER TWENTY-THREE

CONCLUSIONS TO REACH ON ONE'S OWN

I F TODAY, AFTER EVERYTHING I HAVE conveyed about these matters from the perspective of Eternity, one still can seriously ask *what* exactly remains capable of experience in those who have departed, after the death of the physical body, so that this enduring consciousness is able both to seize the hands of helpers from above, but also may reject them, and thus confine itself for immeasurable ages within the phantom *border realms* it had participated in sustaining—I have to ask in turn whether those who yet discern so little, despite everything they read in works of my guidance, are not perhaps merely mechanical reading machines, since they obviously feel no more when reading my words than a gramophone hears the sounds of the record whose grooves its needle is tracing. I certainly know full well that I am forced to find expression for much that can hardly be translated from the realm of Reality into the form of *words*; and I surely am not presumptuous enough to assume that I have found the most perfect rendition for what I needed to say. Beyond any discussion, however, is the fact, countless times proven in practice, that it is possible to reach the right answer from the sense of my words simply by common logic, and thus put to rest any lingering question that still might arise without my having discussed it expressly. Also the query referred to above surely requires no particular keenness of mind to be answered. Besides, it has been done often enough by everything I had to say regarding the continued existence of a consciousness and will after the death of the physical body.

That it is *not* the animal soul of the human mortal on earth which survives the death of the body, surely follows clearly enough from my stating that this animal soul is merely the functional effect of the physical body's existence, and therefore ceases to exist at the death of that body. What may continue to exist for a while are merely figurations that have been called "doppelgänger" or "astral bodies." These figurations are phantoms that the individual's impulse to generate its own forms caused to come into being through the energies of the animal soul, while the latter was still in active existence. As a result of that activity they may survive the dissolution of the animal soul the same length of time as the other physical effects of impulses generated by the animal soul; a great number of these are in fact left behind in the physical sphere as after-effects of every concluded life on earth. As actively effective memories, these phantoms may, while they exist, generate occult spooks and pranks, but they no longer have the least to do with those who once had produced them. What exclusively remains able after the death of the physical body to serve as a bearer of the individuated consciousness of the earthly human being that formerly had been aware of itself in the animal soul, is the enduring *eternal soul*, which in effect still preserves in itself the memory of all the sensible impressions it had been receiving from the human being's animal soul, with which it had once been connected, during the latter's bodily life. Within the timeless soul alone also continues to live the *will* and the *sensibility*, determined on earth, which the mortal human being once had known in its animal soul.

For the eternal soul this condition is doubtless a bondage it would be without the sooner the better. On the other hand, this form of "life after death," such as it needs to be faced until the ultimate liberation of the eternal soul, is still entirely part of *earthly life*. It is simply that period of earthly human life that is to be experienced without the visible animal body, and thus without the animal soul. Not until also this form of earthly life has been completely lived to its end, by exhausting the impulse-driven energies generated during physical life, by use of the animal soul, will the timeless individual soul—formed by eternal energies during life in a physical body, helped by the latter's resonance of sensibility—at last find itself entirely free to preserve from earthly memory what it wants to retain, and to dissolve what it judges unworthy of permanent recollection.

What is to be said in this context, I have in addition expressed in simplest form on the last pages of the small collection of rhythmic verse *Living in Light*; and if here I speak of two different images of the *soul*, one now will surely comprehend that the subject refers to what the animal soul is able to impart to the eternal soul as a memory of permanent presence. The eternal soul can truly never become a "sty," nor a "putrid pool," and as such rot away. Owing to its connection with an animal soul during physical life, however, it is compelled to absorb also sense impressions through the animal soul which at times regrettably call for far more drastic comparisons than those I used for clarification.

There are organizations that seek to prevent the needless suffering of animals, and such endeavors truly deserve every support. No less, however, should humans be attentive to spare their own timeless soul unspeakable burdens, whose weight will oppress them after their temporal life has come to an end.

❧

CHAPTER TWENTY-FOUR

ON CRUCIAL UNDERESTIMATION

ALTHOUGH FOLLOWERS OF VENERABLE ancient religions in whose view the human being on earth seems to consist of merely a mortal body and an immortal soul, might at the most be willing to concede that in their own self-expressions during life on earth something comparable to the *soul* of animals seeks to assert itself, one nonetheless may be sure that those possibly inclined to agree shall accord these manifestations an upper limit of effects, which, in reality, scarcely embraces even the whole of their lowest range. All higher sensations they attribute already to their eternal soul, firmly convinced that only insignificant lower things could find expression in a matrix of life, restricted by time, which itself is in truth merely the functional effect of the impermanent physical body. To a certain degree this understanding is indeed supported by the fact that, in the human being, the animal soul, as already discussed, receives profoundly significant influences from the eternal soul, which guide it in some ways to immeasurably higher levels than are part of its own nature; and these influences are not received by any animal. It has therefore become very difficult to determine with certainty what still must be attributed to the human being's earthly animal soul, and what is without question the effect of that being's enduring soul. At any rate, however, one may at all times be certain that the upper limit of that which is owing to the impermanent, earthly animal soul of the human being in bondage to the earth can never be drawn at too high a level. The reclusive monks of Mount Athos in their own way undoubtedly show profound insight by declaring every form of scholarly learning incompatible with genuine piety, and an obstacle to visions of God. To understand that correctly, however, one must bear in mind that these ascetic anchorites were by no means thinking of merely the commonplace differences between faith and knowledge, but rejected intellectual learning as such, even though it embraced "orthodox" theology, and knowledge of scripture beyond every shadow of religious doubt. Their insight causes them, to be sure in exaggerated reasoning, to regard an illiterate, who devotes his life exclusively to his timeless soul, far more highly than someone familiar with all questions of orthodox theology that can be answered by virtue of the mind; for they know very well that also the latter's intellect owes very much to the influences of the eternal soul, but that his scholarly comprehension scarcely has need of the soul that endures.

Perhaps it may be a shock for some readers of these words to recognize that, confident beyond all doubt, and likely in the best of good faith, they had always ascribed to their eternal soul what now, if they would yield to the truth, they gratefully must henceforth attribute to their temporary, earthly animal soul. But it is better once to confront such a shock than to continue indulging oneself in dreams which correspond so very little with reality, and thus cannot bring forth anything real in those whom dreams hold in bondage. Now it is certainly not necessary, like the strictest among the reclusive monks of Mount Athos, to devote oneself exclusively to the conscious perception of the eternal soul, and to suspect in everything that may reach one's consciousness through the temporal, animal-limited soul, nothing but the "pitfalls of hell." On the contrary, it is appropriate to treat the animal soul in oneself with profoundest respect, and by no means to deem of little worth what it is able to convey to the human being on earth. The goal to strive for, however, is wholly to submit the animal-bound soul to the service of the eternal soul; for thus it may further the work of the latter in ways one could hardly imagine. While the animal soul is not, unlike the enduring soul, the self-aware realm of experience for an individuated, timeless scintilla of the Spirit—nor will reveal itself in sensible form of highest primordial energies, which are capable of illumination—it is nonetheless a *secondary* effect of primordial Being, even though in the latter's Self-manifestation farthest from Light, where it only generates blindly, as the source which everything given form in the universe owes, and continues to owe its structure. One here is well advised to show profound respect, and any kind of underestimation is bound to have undesirable consequences.

To be sure, those who believe in the existence of an eternal soul, or perhaps already think they can feel its presence, may well be displeased to be told that even the highest achievements of human thinking—whether reached in the discipline commonly called "philosophy," or in religion, mathematics, and any fields of the most highly developed technology, including chemistry, and medical research—can most certainly be attained without the slightest involvement of a person's eternal soul. Still more difficult will they find it to grasp that even technically highly proficient works in all fields of art are in truth solely products of the animal soul, which has reached its highest development in the human being. At any level of technical value, however, such works may doubtless become creations in which the eternal soul finds expression. There is hardly another word more thoroughly abused than the concept of "soul," which even those would want to see accepted as a term for something superior to mere animal nature, who most resolutely would consider it an imposition were they expected to rank the *reality* of the eternal soul above their mentally constructed phantom view of the world.

&

CHAPTER TWENTY-FIVE

ON THE
DILEMMA OF
PASTORAL CARE

Fᴿᴼᴹ ᴛɪᴍᴇ ᴛᴏ ᴛɪᴍᴇ ɪ ꜱᴛɪʟʟ ᴋᴇᴇᴘ ɢᴇᴛᴛɪɴɢ letters sent by readers remarkably well acquainted with my books who feel compelled to vent their indignation or dismay concerning some dismissive, foolish, or categorically rejecting utterances about my writings made by a professional representative of a religious faith with whom they are acquainted. One brings the like to my attention assuming that I welcome to be kept informed, so that I might defend myself against such slighting judgments, either privately or in public. Yet such a view is prompted by an optimism I am quite unable to share. One fails to bear in mind that the official leaders of a religious association, whatever historically evolved titles they may rightfully hold, and though their association may prefer to call itself a "church," which believes itself to be endowed with God-given spiritual powers, remain in every instance appointed officials of that creedal association, and as such are under obligation to protect its interests. But no official of any church, nor any scholar choosing to serve the interests of an association bound by a common creed, has the slightest obligation whatever thoughtfully to read my writings for the sake of personal benefit. If these books should happen to come into their hands, one certainly cannot hold it against them if they regard their content with instinctive suspicion. The more confined in perspective, and insecure in belief, the more superficial, as a result, will also be their view of these writings; and the more surely, therefore, will they fear their contents would threaten the interests of the institution to which they owe their position, dignity, title, and livelihood; a denomination that, after all, represents also a doctrine of faith that, in their belief, offers eternal salvation to the faithful who feel drawn to its teachings. No wonder they would see the flock entrusted to their care protected from expositions that at times do not *sound* like the literal meaning of the doctrine they are bound to present to their followers. Such leaders of a religious congregation, or their confession-bound theologians, would have to be exceedingly farseeing representatives of their profession, endowed with remarkably mature judgment, if after reading some of my writings they were to realize what the latter contain. Indeed, that the dissemination and proof of what they believe—and which, according to their religious conviction, is the correct thing to believe—could not find a mightier source of help than is offered in the contents of these writings. Yet nearly all such shepherds of souls, whom I am far from holding in low esteem, are in their minds inseparably chained both to the *literal* text known to them of the doctrines in which they believe, as well as to the *interpretation* of the words that, traditionally, count as the classical doctrine of theology. Given such contrary certainty of opinion, how could I presume there merely was need of some elucidation, or possibly an irrefutable rectification, in order to bring about the liberation of a pastor held in such bondage? For none of those in this situation even suspects that, together with all the unassailable truth, they also are spreading serious errors among people. On the other hand, it could never even occur to me to insist upon being "right," since what I convey is not subject to any earthly evaluation. I bring knowledge from the realm of the Eternal, which can be conveyed solely by one who, owing to his spiritual Being, is spiritually anchored in the Eternal.

Respecting the reviled clerics, however, of whom one rather naively expects they joyfully ought to welcome what is offered them in my writings, one tends to forget that they are mortal human beings, and that the "spirit" to which they have dedicated themselves is a creation of the brain, even though it may occupy itself with problems of religion. How can one expect that servants of the cerebral spirit should be able to recognize what has its roots in the Spirit that is timeless? But I most certainly do not in any way blame the servants of the mental spirit in official religions for their judgment. The entire "spiritual" education they received was structured in such a way that they could not possibly harbor the slightest doubt of having the Spirit within them. How should they now, after reading publications of a "layman," find themselves convinced that to this day they had been victims of self-deception?

Nor could I possibly agree to regard the employment status of pastors serving a religious community as being responsible for the intransigent attitude respecting my works offering trustworthy knowledge. For all the clearly determined positions that teachers of religion are obliged to observe, there is not in practice anything like the rigidly confining oppression of personal opinion, as presumed by outsiders, uninformed of all things pertaining to churches. To be sure, also among the teaching officials of the various faiths one may find the same pompous self-importance and narrow-minded arrogance one at times will encounter in other types of officialdom. But while in the course of my life I have come into close personal contact with not a few representatives of the religious associations existing in Europe, I very rarely have met with such pharisaic self-righteousness. On the contrary, I nearly always found a most genuine dedication to the accepted responsibility for the spiritual well-being of the souls entrusted to their care; together with a remarkable readiness to be helpful to those in need. And thus I truly value the life-work of those here referred to by no means any less, whether they feel sympathetically drawn to my disclosures from the Eternal, or be it that misunderstanding, and the pressure of their responsibility, caused them to feel compelled rather to warn against reading them.

It also is greatly mistaken to assume that one already has begun with understanding to approach the emanation of the Eternal, present in my mere existence, and at the same time in the teachings conveyed in earthly human form, as long as one has not yet even grasped that I could not deny its right to exist to any authentic form of religion I encounter on earth. Yet on the other hand one should no less be aware that the Spirit's eternal powers have never employed the official representatives of existing religious corporations whenever particular regions of humanity were meant to receive new insights into Eternity, from the Eternal. The global religions, whose believers today count in the millions, had without exception received the initial impulse that led to their founding by *outsiders*. From the ranks of the official organizations of priests, preachers, and shepherds caring for souls, have never emerged more than *reformers* of existing conditions. What in my Guidance is given on earth from the Eternal, and left for those yet to come, is not, however, intended to effect new religious reforms, nor the founding of new religions. Once being recognized, where it is needed, in the life of the soul, it will instead rather confirm the innermost truth concealed in all religions inspired by the Eternal, no less than the necessity of their various forms, also willed by the Eternal, to which the human founders or initiators gave physical expression for mortals on earth.

☙

CHAPTER TWENTY-SIX

HOW EVERYTHING ETERNAL IS TO ITSELF MERELY *NATURAL*

F ROM NOT A FEW OF THE UNSOLICITED letters sent to me since the first of my books were published, I was compelled to conclude *ad nauseam* that readers naively imagined a temporal interpreter of the Eternal on earth to be shockingly different from what he could here in reality possibly be as a *spiritual* Mediator. Too many images of antiquated religious romanticism still spook about in modern minds; and too much golden tinsel has, for thousands, or at least hundreds of years, glittered around the human beings who were able to be guides for their fellow mortals, to lead them to the timeless reality of the Spirit's radiant substance. As a result, many even today are unwilling readily to give up what long has been close to their heart, for the sake of *Reality*, which has at all times been far simpler, more attuned to the earth, than mere fantasizing, and the need for fairy tale trappings are prepared to accept. Thus, even those for whom alone my books have been written, so that through my words they were able to find the path to Life and Light, often have great difficulty in their joy and gratitude, to let me simply be a human being among and like others. They do not bear in mind that what is *truly eternal* can reveal itself only in what is truly *natural*, given that to the Eternal its being *eternal* is perfectly *natural*. The grandiose gesture and the craving for nimbus have through the ages been the most telling signs of that which in humans is not genuine within itself; for the truly genuine does not owe its life to the impression it makes upon others, but lives instead through its own genuine essence.

The creation of romanticizing legends—which at all times was able to take root and flourish wherever on earth a human being lived who could bring to his fellow mortals certainty about the truly *eternal* within them—unquestionably shows everywhere countless malformations of growth, and scars of foolish grafting, but its value is nonetheless high; for it protected many a testimony from the

Eternal, of which, lacking such overgrowth, no trace would have survived to this day in the general awareness of humanity. Less grateful, however, must one be to the elegiac, or lyrically enthused biographers of those who spoke from their own eternal identity, or had gained inspiration from the Eternal through some other spiritual path; voices whose insights are still faintly preserved today under the covering thicket of many a legend. For it is to those biographers one has to attribute the portraits that distorted unpretentious and natural men, whose conscious self-awareness was illuminated from the Eternal, and turned them into figures of fantasy, grossly unnatural and untrue, because the writers could not tame their imagination, and knew of neither the secret of pure human simplicity, which was beyond their grasp, nor realized how close to the earth abides the Divine.

For every single believer whom excessive zeal in early days was able to convert, out of a naïvely uncritical multitude, through unnatural exaggerations and invented additions, thousands today must sacrifice their faith, until one learns to distinguish what once had been a human life's reality, and what exalted missionary fanaticism judged it necessary to compose from it.

Given my earthly roots of flesh and blood, I most certainly am not by nature blasphemous enough to invite "comparison," even from the remotest distance, with any of the here depicted, in grossest measure distorted figures; and one surely has no idea how little I think of expressions of reverence, in pious aberration coined anew, yet now with my image, although they betray only too clearly that their source is a mint whose gold is polluted with verdigris. Wherever the gold is genuine, however, its coinage shows me—in each and every case—invariably the image of a human being *connected* with God, *united with* God, or fervently *conscious* of God within; and that image I venerate far too highly in each instance to let its natural features be distorted, imposing on them a spurious "resemblance," neither reflecting myself, nor the one portrayed in the past. Quite apart from that, in the Eternal, there neither is found *uniformity*, nor *repetition*. The Eternal has at all times become manifest in unique and singular form in the human being on earth; nor would it ever have need to *copy* itself. Furthermore, the

Eternal remains in itself beyond all veneration; and wherever human beings believed they were "honoring" the manifestation of the Divine in one of their fellow mortals, they honored in truth—solely themselves, and their own timeless *human* essence, whose nature at times is able, in unique individuals, to bear the Eternal within it, and of its manifest Self to be conscious.

Someone devoid of humor, for instance, is certainly not at any time close to God, even if to those around him he may appear as the purest source of divine revelation. A lively sense of joyful humor is far too much part of the essential self-recognition of the Eternal, for its being able to manifest itself in a mortal who is a misfit from birth, being drawn toward things dismal and gloomy, and thus incapable of sharing God-given laughter. To be sure, this component of the Eternal has nothing to do with mockery and wit, however much these may stimulate physical laughter. If thus one assumes that someone who is able to convey knowledge of God would have to be trembling in a state of perpetual seriousness, one is simply mistaken. It is very much worth one's while clearly to recognize this error as such.

Despite his bent toward mischief and *schaden-freude*, Wilhelm Busch* was truly far closer to the Eternal than the ascetic hermit of the Theban desert, whom he ridiculed battling against the devil's temptations.

Furthermore, every guide who could speak of God with authority was a child of his age, spoke the language of his time, bore its burdens, dressed in the style of his country, ate and drank with others as was the custom of his land, without fear of committing a sin when in his physical body he fully experienced the body's effects. Whatever in ancient records presents a different picture has been added by zealous enthusiasts, who in this way sought to furnish the object of their veneration, whose reality eluded their grasp, with the nimbus of the *supernatural*, because they knew nothing of how being *natural* is the essence of all things Divine. They did not realize that what they took to be *supernatural* was but the invention and refuge of their own *unnatural* manner, since also the realm tran-

---

*Wilhelm Busch (1832-1908), celebrated painter and poet, whose humorous drawings and verse satirized contemporary philistinism and religious bigotry.—*trans.*

scending the physical can become known to only what likewise is *natural*.

And so I hope one may learn to understand that even though I am forced to presuppose *extraordinary* discernment, and have to speak of matters that *transcend* temporal life, that the Eternal of which I speak through my temporal voice, is nonetheless to me the most *natural* part of my Being. And indeed, also my contemporaries, when speaking, as is their common practice, of the "supernatural," in fact mean rather the "super-physical," which to me is a *natural* sphere of life, no less than the earthly domain, which I negate in no form whatever, but love from the view of Eternity. I know full well that the condition of consciousness that grew to be my own, imparted by the Eternal—in timeless primordial Light, in the spiritual human being of Eternity, as well as in the physically short-lived, animal-embodied mortal on earth—appears to my fellow mortals on earth as alien and strange, as this state is unknown to their own consciousness. Besides, humans have for thousands of years sought in good faith to convince each other that only something "supernatural" could be capable of consciously living at once in the temporal and the eternal domain. My own earthly constitution did not by any means make it easy for me to learn to understand my primordially given state of consciousness also in my mental awareness; and not a day passes even now when my temporal self might not have still more to learn from within the Eternal. As a heavy, but necessary burden, I had to overcome, even from early youth, a physically inherited, utterly active trait of self-criticism, as well as a bent toward inexorable skepticism, which caused me much anguish embracing the faith I was taught in my youth. In addition, I later gained insight, which by contrast provided relief, into all physically rooted events that in common scientific termi-nology are referred to as "psychic"; events that may lead to erroneous explanations in mental understanding, and thus are able to cast their spell upon even those having merit in drawing attention to this hidden domain. In view of all this I am certainly able, based on my own experience, to judge with sympathetic understanding every conceivable attitude re-specting my spiritual disclosures, as well as for all erroneous notions regarding myself. Precisely for that reason, however, am I no stranger—within the Eternal—even to those among my fellow mortals on earth who most firmly reject the things I convey. Perhaps I am much closer to them than their earthly awareness is apt to suspect?

To state that the Eternal is in essence *natural* does not imply, however, its indifference to *form*. All, therefore, who do not care whether they—wherever it be—respect, or offend against, form must clearly bear in mind that acting thus they *isolate* themselves from everything truly Eternal, which wants to gain form throughout all existence, and will reveal itself in the innermost only of those seeking to form themselves, both in their inner and outer existence, to become vessels serving the Godhead.

❧

CHAPTER TWENTY-SEVEN

CONCLUSION
AND
FAREWELL

WITH THIS BOOK I CONCLUDE MY temporal work of Spiritual Guidance. Soon after the beginning of the twentieth century, according to the Christian era, I undertook to put into words the first insights which had at that time become my mental understanding's possession, conveyed through the Self I am in the Spirit. What I had set down in this way remained untouched for years, since initially I had no intention at all to make it public myself during the lifespan allotted me on earth. Not until 1912 and 1913 came the first manuscripts of the now published texts into being, at various sites in Greece, occasioned by external and inner experiences of a singular kind, to which I refer in various contexts of my writings. Already in 1910, however, I had become convinced that it was necessary personally to publish during my lifetime what I had written, and thus had from then on accordingly worded particular sections. In 1913, submitted from Athens, where it still was revised several times, such a fragment appeared for the first time in print. Now, in the stormy days of 1936, I conclude my literary work of Spiritual Guidance, which encloses all, but nothing other than, the titles explicitly listed after the last words of this book, which completes the cycle of texts that begins with *The Book on the Royal Art*.

Thus, the essays on the visual arts I combined in *Reflections on the Realm of Art*, as well as the more biographically intended pamphlet *"In My Own Behalf,"* and the small work *Views from My Studio*, which also is chiefly biographical, are not, of course, part of my works of Spiritual Guidance, although they display its traces. The same is true of *Enigmas of Nature's Invisible Realm*. Any separately published essays I have not until today included in one of my books are likewise not to form part of my now completed Spiritual Guidance, although this exclusion is not retroactively to diminish their value. Under no circumstances, however, must any passage in private letters I have not myself included in one of the books of the now completed cycle of teachings be considered at any time as being part of my Guidance, or be employed to interpret one of its sections. I can accept eternal responsibility for nothing other than solely the content, as presented today, of the books openly published that are listed below. In respect to letters not published by me I bear no other responsibility, even where they touch on spiritual matters, than purely that incurred at the time, customary in human relationships, which demands no more of an utterance than that it express what someone, in the course of everyday life, feels prompted to say at the moment, and only concerning the moment. I have never written letters meant for "posterity," but was always led by willingness to help the respective writers, even when I was by no means certain they deserved such concern. Disappointments painful to bear I surely was not spared in this effort.

The foregoing is not to imply that I now commit myself to publish no other books in future, regardless of their subject. In advance, however, I must reject the idea of treating anything I might still feel obliged to express as if it were part of my Spiritual Guidance, which has now been completed. This closure is not determined by personal choice, but respects the demand of the task here concluded.

The series of works in which this Spiritual Guidance has now been published in definitive form, will nonetheless remain a *Hortus Conclusus*—a securely enclosed *Gated Garden* —barred to all of my fellow mortals who would find in it anything other than their own *eternal* nature; and barred it will remain, even if the narrow portal offering entrance has widely been opened before them. Nothing is farther from my purpose than seeking that those gain admittance who are not welcomed to enter, or to give guidance within it to any that must stay without. The more gladly, however, I send my blessings to all who serenely leave their earthly being at its rightful place, and in my Spiritual Guidance seek only their timeless self. I do not provide systematized instructions, but guidance embodying life. The thirty-two individual works, comprising as many parts of my Spiritual Guidance, contain everything humans on earth need to know of eternal life, and of the relationships connecting them with the Eternal, given that finding its entrance within themselves is their earnest resolve, so that one day they may become able to experience existence within the Eternal. There is great danger in becoming so deeply entangled in physical life that the ability to sense the Eternal may never be attained. What suffers harm thereby is not the Eternal, but human mortals as earthly beings, who thereby forfeit, completely and irrevocably, what is *eternal* in their nature, without the slightest sense of awareness. Countless such separations of the human being's *earthly* consciousness from the *eternal*, which it latently possesses, are taking place day after day, every single hour. To rescue more than religions today are able to save is the reason my Spiritual Guidance came into being. My *successor*—a human being in the same spiritual situation as mine, and like myself appointed to serve as a perceptible voice on earth of the primordial Word—will keep numerable cycles of generations waiting for his arrival, and not appear on earth to offer further direction on the path I have shown, until what I have written in this now completed Guidance has become knowledge universally shared in mind and soul by all on earth who strive to find the Eternal.

Only one does not receive the spiritual life conveyed through my words by restlessly turning them over in one's mind, nor by discussions with others, or in one's own head, concerning the intellectually discernible content of the thirty-two separate parts of this Guidance. Instead, one has to be willing, free of compulsive mental probing, to receive them, and their effect on oneself, in the form they now have been given; for otherwise one cannot learn even to fathom and sense the life that is offered within them, whose origin is the Eternal. Those who once have in themselves become aware of this—my own life in the Spirit—conveyed in my words, and then have received and sensed it within, shall thus be liberated of all doubt, which is the bane that haunts the fear of mistaken conclusions in any mind that misuses its gift of rational thinking for the sake of constructing lanes from mental debris, deluded by the notion that following them one ought to be able to reach timeless Reality.

❧

DEFINITIVE LISTING
OF MY SPIRITUAL
GUIDANCE

1.

THE BOOK ON THE ROYAL ART
(1932 edition)

The "Royal Art" referred to in this book is the Indian Raja Yoga; but here I use the term only symbolically to signify something immeasurably superior.

Light from Himavat and Words of the Masters

The Luminary's Self-Disclosure to the Seeking Soul. The Harvest. The ONE whose Being is Infinity. Know Thyself. On the Masters of the Spirit's World. Pitfalls of Vanity.

From the Lands of the Luminaries

The Threshold. The King's Question. The Pillar in the Mountains. The Night of Easter. Communion.

The Will to Joy

*To All who strive toward Timeless Light.
The Teachings On Joy. Epilogue.*

2.

THE BOOK ON THE LIVING GOD
(1927 edition)

Word of Guidance. "The Tabernacle of God is with Men." The White Lodge. Meta-Physical Experiences. The Inner Journey.

The En-Sof. On Seeking God. On Leading an Active Life. On "Holy Men" and "Sinners." The Hidden Side of Nature. The Secret Temple. Karma. War and Peace. The Unity among Religions. The Will to Find Eternal Light. The Human Being's Higher Faculties of Knowing. On Death. On the Spirit's Radiant Substance. The Path toward Perfection. On Everlasting Life. The Spirit's Light Dwells in the East. Faith, Talismans, and Images of God. The Inner Force in Words. A Call from Himavat. Giving Thanks. Epilogue.

3.

THE BOOK ON LIFE BEYOND
(1929 edition)

Introduction. The Art of Dying. The Temple of Eternity and the World of Spirit. The Only Absolute Reality. What Should One Do?

4.

THE BOOK ON HUMAN NATURE
(1928 edition)

Introduction. The Mystery Enshrouding Male and Female. The Path of the Female. The Path of the Male. Marriage. Children. The Human Being of the Age to Come. Epilogue. A Final Word.

5.

THE BOOK ON HAPPINESS

Prelude. Creating Happiness as Moral Duty. "I" and "You." Love. Wealth and Poverty. Money. Optimism. Conclusion.

6.

THE PATH TO GOD

Fantasy and Faith. Knowing Certainty. Dreaming Souls. Truth and Reality. Yes and No. The Decisive Battle. Individual Perfection.

7.

THE BOOK ON LOVE

Introduction. The Greatest of Compassion's Mediators. On Love's Primordial Fire. Light of Liberation. On Love's Creative Power.

8.

THE BOOK ON SOLACE

On Grief and Finding Solace. Lessons One can Learn from Grief. On Follies to Avoid. On the Comforting Virtue of Work. On Solace in Bereavement.

9.

THE BOOK OF DIALOGUES

Testimony. Knowledge and Reality in Action. Light and Darkness. The Spirit's Might. The Jewel of the Heart. Transformation. The Dialogue on the Innermost East. The Dialogue on the Passing of a Master. The Flower Garden. The Deviant Pupils. Night of Trial. Individuality and Person. The Realm of the Soul. On Finding Oneself. On the Elder Brothers of Humankind. Mysteries of Magic.

10.

THE SECRET

Beginning. The Discourse by the Shore. The Monastery of San Spirito. Southern Night. The Island of the Rock. The Voyage on the Sea. Epilogue.

11.

THE WISDOM OF ST. JOHN

Introduction. The Master's Image. The Luminary's Mortal Life. The Aftermath. The Missive. The Authentic Doctrine. The Paraclete. Conclusion.

12.
SIGNS ALONG THE WAY

Promise. Experience and Phenomenon. On Knowing and Conveying Knowledge. The Art of Reading. On Letters. Personality Cult. Compulsive Criticizing. Who was Jakob Böhme? The Gift of Healing. Dangers of Mysticism. Twenty-two texts in verse.

13.
THE MIRAGE OF TRUE FREEDOM.

Fata Morgana. Necessity. Community. Authority. Divisiveness. Economic Mismanagement. Competition. Slogan Mania. Self-Expression. Religion. Science. On Being Conscious of Reality.

14.
THE PATH OF MY PUPILS

Whom I Consider My Pupil. Critical Distinctions. Needless Self-Torment. Unavoidable Difficulties. Dynamic Faith. The Greatest Obstacle. Pupils and Their Companions. Inner Life and Outer World. How One Ought to Use My Books.

15.
THE MYSTERY OF GOLGOTHA

Introduction. The Mystery of Golgotha. The Most Pernicious of Our Foes. Love and Hatred. The Soul and Its Growth. Spiritual Guidance. Occultists' Exercises. Mediumism and Artistic Creation. At the Wellspring of Life. Membership in the "White Lodge." Follies of Imagination.

16.
CEREMONIAL MAGIC AND MYTH

Preface. Humanity's Creative Works. Myth and Reality. Myth and Ritual. Ritual as Form of Magic. Magic and Spiritual Cognition. The Inner Light. Conclusions One Should Draw.

17.

THE MEANING OF THIS LIFE

A Call to the Lost. The Iniquity of the Fathers. The Highest Good. The "Evil" Individual. Summons from the World of Light. The Benefits of Silence. Truth and Verities. Conclusion.

18.

MORE LIGHT

Preface. Words of Guidance. To All Those Tired of Sleeping. The Builders of Humanity's Eternal Temple. Theosophy and Pseudotheosophy. Matter, Soul, and Spirit. What Must Be Understood. The Mystery of Artistic Expression. The Kabbalah. The Spirit's Light Within Christianity. The Secret of the Ancient Lodges. On Real Worship.

19.

LIFE'S HIGHEST GOAL

The Call of the Spirit. The Two Paths. On Seeking and Finding. The Radiance of Eternal Light. The Colors of Eternal Light. On the Nature of the Highest Goal. On the Paths of the Ancients. On the Blessings of Work. The Might of Love. The Master of Nazareth.

20.

RESURRECTION

Preface. Resurrection. The Knowledge of Sages. Effects of Law and Chance. Wasted labors. Mardi Gras of the Occult. Inner Voices. The Magic Effect of Fear. The Limits of Omnipotence. The New Life. Festive Joy. The Virtue of Laughter. Self-Conquest. Conclusion.

21.

WORLDS OF SPIRIT

Preface. The Ascent. The Return. Reviews of Creation. Epilogue.
(This book contains 20 color reproductions of my paintings.)

22.

PSALMS

Inferno. Deliverance. Insight. Assurance.
Liberation. Fulfillment.

23.

ON MARRIAGE

The Timeless Sanctity of Marriage. On Love. On Sharing Life.
On Joy and Sorrow. On Temptation and Danger. The Con-
straints of Daily Life. The Will to Seek Unity. On Happiness
as Heritage. On Everlasting Union.

24.

ON PRAYER

The Mystery of Praying. "Seek, and You Shall Find." "Ask,
and You Shall Receive." "Knock, and It Shall Be Opened
Unto You." Spiritual Renewal. Let This Be Your
Prayer: Twenty-two Prayers.

25.

SPIRIT AND FORM

The Question. Outer World and Inner Life. At Home and at
Work. Forming one's Joy. Forming One's Grief.
The Art of Living.

26.

SCINTILLAS.
(German Mantras)
Includes the brief exposition The Use Of Mantras.

27.

WORDS OF LIFE

A Call to You. Myself. Turning Inward. Love. Action. Struggle.
Peace. Strength. Life. Light. Trust. Illumination. Avowal.

28.
ABOVE THE EVERYDAY
Thirty-four poems of Guidance. Part One.

29.
ETERNAL REALITY
Twenty-seven poems of Guidance. Part Two.

30.
LIFE WITHIN LIGHT
Thirty-two poems of Guidance. Part Three.

31.
LETTERS TO ONE AND MANY
*Thirty chapters written as letters, including eighteen poems.
Conclusion.*

32.
THE GATED GARDEN
*The present volume of the Cycle, comprising the twenty-seven
chapters listed on the table of Contents.*

**Massagno, Switzerland
Summer 1936
Bô Yin Râ
(Joseph Anton Schneiderfranken)**

REMINDER

"Yet here I must point out again that if one would derive the fullest benefit from studying the books I wrote to show the way into the Spirit, one has to read them in the original; even if this should require learning German.

"Translations can at best provide assistance in helping readers gradually perceive, even through the spirit of a different language, what I convey with the resources of my mother tongue."

From "Answers to Everyone" (1933),
Gleanings. Bern: Kobersche Verlags-
buchhandlung, 1990

THE
KOBER
PRESS